Writing and Script: A Very Short Introduction

VERY SHORT INTRODUCTIONS are for anyone wanting a stimulating and accessible way into a new subject. They are written by experts, and have been translated into more than 45 different languages.

The series began in 1995, and now covers a wide variety of topics in every discipline. The VSI library now contains over 500 volumes—a Very Short Introduction to everything from Psychology and Philosophy of Science to American History and Relativity—and continues to grow in every subject area.

Titles in the series include the following:

Andrew Robinson

WRITING AND SCRIPT

A Very Short Introduction

OXFORD
UNIVERSITY PRESS

OXFORD
UNIVERSITY PRESS

Great Clarendon Street, Oxford OX2 6DP

Oxford University Press is a department of the University of Oxford.
It furthers the University's objective of excellence in research, scholarship,
and education by publishing worldwide in

Oxford New York

Auckland Cape Town Dar es Salaam Hong Kong Karachi
Kuala Lumpur Madrid Melbourne Mexico City Nairobi
New Delhi Shanghai Taipei Toronto

With offices in

Argentina Austria Brazil Chile Czech Republic France Greece
Guatemala Hungary Italy Japan Poland Portugal Singapore
South Korea Switzerland Thailand Turkey Ukraine Vietnam

Oxford is a registered trade mark of Oxford University Press
in the UK and in certain other countries

Published in the United States
by Oxford University Press Inc., New York

British Library Cataloguing in Publication Data
Data available

Library of Congress Cataloging in Publication Data
Data available

Typeset by SPI Publisher Services, Pondicherry, India
Printed and bound by
CPI Group (UK) Ltd, Croydon, CR0 4YY

ISBN 978-0-19-956778-2

Contents

Acknowledgements

This is the fourth book I have written on writing and scripts. The first was a highly illustrated survey of the subject, the second was on undeciphered scripts, and the third was a biography of Michael Ventris, who deciphered Europe's earliest readable writing, Linear B. I have also written a biography of the polymath Thomas Young, a key figure in the decipherment of the Rosetta Stone and Egyptian hieroglyphic.

On the way, I have accumulated many debts to current specialists in the various scripts, who freely gave me advice. Some of their expert knowledge has found its way into this small book. Although they had nothing directly to do with it, I would particularly like to recall the help of John Baines, John Bennet, Larissa Bonfante, the late John Chadwick, Michael Coe, Robert Englund, Jacques Guy, Stephen Houston, Kim Juwon, Oliver Moore, Tom Palaima, Asko Parpola, and J. Marshall Unger.

It is a pleasure to thank Andrea Keegan, Latha Menon, and Keira Dickinson of Oxford University Press.

List of illustrations

Chapter 1
Writing and its emergence

Civilization cannot exist without spoken language, but it can without written communication. The Greek poetry of Homer was at first transmitted orally, stored in the memory, as were the Vedas, the Sanskrit hymns of the ancient Hindus, which were unwritten for centuries. The South American empire of the Incas managed its administration without writing. Yet eventually, almost every complex society – ancient and modern – has required a script or scripts. Writing, though not obligatory, is a defining marker of civilization. Without writing, there can be no accumulation of knowledge, no historical record, no science (though simple technology may exist), and of course no books, newspapers, emails, or World Wide Web.

The creation of writing in Mesopotamia (present-day Iraq) and Egypt in the late 4th millennium BC permitted the command and seal of a ruler like the Babylonian Hammurabi, the Roman Julius Caesar, or the Mongol Kublai Khan, to extend far beyond his sight and voice and even to survive his death. If the Rosetta Stone had never been inscribed, for example, the world would be virtually unaware of the nondescript Graeco-Egyptian king Ptolemy V Epiphanes, whose priests promulgated his decree upon the Rosetta Stone in 196 BC written in three scripts: sacred hieroglyphic, administrative demotic, and Greek alphabetic.

Writing and literacy are generally seen as forces for good. All modern parents want their children to be able to read and write. But there is a negative side to the spread of writing that is present throughout its more than 5,000-year history, if somewhat less obvious. In the 5th century BC, the Greek philosopher Socrates (who famously never published a word) pinpointed our ambivalence towards 'visible speech' in his story of the Egyptian god Thoth, the mythical inventor of writing. Thoth came to see the king seeking royal blessing on his enlightening invention. But instead of praising it, the king told Thoth:

> You have invented an elixir not of memory, but of reminding; and you offer your pupils the appearance of wisdom, not true wisdom, for they will read many things without instruction and will therefore seem to know many things, when they are for the most part ignorant.

In a 21st-century world saturated with written information and surrounded by information technologies of astonishing speed, convenience, and power, these words of Socrates recorded by his disciple Plato have a distinctly contemporary ring.

This book introduces the origins of writing; the routes via which writing spread and developed into hundreds of scripts for some of the world's thousands of spoken languages; the ways in which different writing systems convey meaning through phonetic signs for consonants, vowels, and syllables, combined with logograms – non-phonetic signs standing for words (for instance, @, $, &, =, ?); the tools and materials that scribes and others have used for writing; the purposes to which writing has been put by societies over five millennia; and the extinction and decipherment of scripts.

Naturally, not every script can be included: a recent academic reference book, *The World's Writing Systems*, runs to almost a thousand substantial pages. However, every significant script is mentioned. For all the enormous variety of scripts, past and present, it turns out that extinct ancient scripts such as Egyptian hieroglyphs, Mesopotamian cuneiform, and Mayan glyphs have much in common in both their structure and function with our modern scripts and our specialized communication systems – whether these be alphabets, Chinese characters, mobile phone text messages, or airport signage. The signs of these scripts and systems may differ vastly from each other, but the linguistic principles behind the signs are similar. The ancient scripts are not dead letters, not just esoteric curiosities. Fundamentally, the way that writers write at the start of the 3rd millennium AD is not different from the way that the ancient Egyptians and Mesopotamians wrote.

Proto-writing and full writing

In a cave at Peche Merle, in Lot, in southern France, there is a boulder with some mysterious signs on it: a stencilled hand – with four splayed fingers and a thumb clearly visible – in red dye, and next to it a random pattern of some eleven red dots. What makes these signs significant is that they are probably 20,000 years old, belonging to the last Ice Age, like many other graffiti from southern France, which often include animal images with signs written over or around them. An example from a different cave shows an engraved figure of a horse, over-engraved with a series of 'P' signs (one of them reversed); in an adjoining cave a horse figure is surrounded by more than 80 'P' signs, many of which clearly were made with different tools.

Are the hand-with-dots and the 'P' signs to be regarded as writing? It is tempting to imagine that the former signs are the palaeolithic equivalent of 'I was here, with my animals' (one dot per animal), and that the latter were made by an Ice Age individual as part of some continuing act of worship. No one knows for sure. Undoubtedly, though, the signs were meant to communicate something.

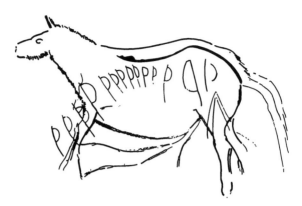

1. This engraved horse, over-engraved with a series of signs, from the cave Les Trois Frères in southern France, dates from the last Ice Age. It is one of many such examples of proto-writing

We can call them 'proto-writing': permanent visible marks capable of partial/specialized communication. Some scholars limit proto-writing to the earliest forms of writing, but in this book the term is applied much more widely. Thus there are endless varieties of proto-writing. It includes prehistoric petroglyphs from around the world, Pictish symbol stones from Scotland, Amerindian pictograms, notched and inscribed wooden tally sticks (used until 1834 by the British Treasury), and the fascinating knotted-rope *quipus* used to keep track of the movement of goods in the Inca empire. Equally valid as proto-writing are contemporary sign systems like international transportation symbols, computer icons, electronic circuit diagrams, mathematical notation, and the staff notation of musical scores.

In other words, the 'proto' prefix refers here not to historical but to functional development. Although proto-writing long preceded the emergence of 'full writing', such as the English alphabet or the Chinese characters, in time, it will always exist alongside full writing. Proto-writing did not disappear as a result of the appearance of full writing – swept away as primitive in some supposed evolutionary progress towards our current superior form of writing – but has continued to be used for specialized purposes. Scientific journals, for instance, contain a mixture of full writing (text generally in alphabetic script) and proto-writing (mathematics and visual diagrams). Theoretically, the mathematics could be expressed in words, as early natural philosophers like Newton often did, but the converse does not hold: the words could not be written in mathematical symbols.

Full writing has been concisely defined as a 'system of graphic symbols that can be used to convey any and all thought' by John DeFrancis, a distinguished American student of Chinese, in his book *Visible Speech: The Diverse Oneness of Writing Systems*. Not all scholars of writing agree with this. A small minority do not draw a distinction between proto-writing and full writing; they regard both of these as 'writing', though capable of differing degrees of expressiveness. Others take issue with the idea that all thought can be expressed in spoken language, and would prefer 'any and all *language*' in the above definition. The most thought-provoking moments in cinema, for example, are often wordless; and mathematicians apparently think more in visual images than in words. Nevertheless, almost all thoughts can be verbalized with sufficient training. 'To know how to write well is to know how to think well', said the mathematician, physicist, and philosopher Blaise Pascal. And so the DeFrancis definition is useful, both in itself and in the way that it implicitly distinguishes full writing from proto-writing.

Clay 'tokens'

One kind of proto-writing that has attracted much attention – because it may provide evidence for the origin of full writing – is the so-called clay 'token'. Archaeological excavations in the Middle East over the past century or so have yielded, besides clay tablets, large numbers of small, unimpressive clay objects. Excavators had no idea what they were, and generally discarded them as worthless. According to the stratigraphy of their excavations, the objects date from 8000 BC – the beginnings of agriculture – to as late as 1500 BC, although the number of finds dated after 3000 BC tails off. The earlier objects are undecorated and geometrically shaped – spheres, cones, and so on, while the later ones are often incised and shaped in more complex ways.

No one can be certain of their function. The most probable explanation, widely accepted, is that they were units in accountancy. Different shapes could have been used to count different entities, such as a sheep from a flock, or a specified measure of a certain product, such as a bushel of grain. The number and variety of shapes could have been extended so that one object of a particular shape could stand for, say, ten sheep or 100 sheep, or black sheep as opposed to white ones. This would have permitted large numbers and amounts to be manipulated arithmetically with comparatively small numbers of clay objects. It would also explain the noticeable trend towards greater complexity of object over time, as the ancient economies ramified.

On these assumptions, the objects are generally termed 'tokens', because they are thought to have represented concepts and quantities. According to one theory, this token system was pictographic writing in embryo; hence the decline in numbers of tokens with the growth of writing on clay tablets after 3000 BC during the 3rd millennium. The substitution of the three-dimensional tokens by two-dimensional symbols on clay tablets was supposedly a first step towards writing. However, although this theory has been much discussed, it is not widely accepted.

To understand why, we need to look at the most interesting among the finds of clay tokens. These show the tokens enclosed in a clay envelope, generally shaped as a hollow ball and known as a 'bulla' (Latin for 'bubble'). Some 80 bullae are known to exist with the tokens intact. Shake the bulla, and the tokens rattle inside it; their outlines are visible using X-rays. The sealed outer surface may carry impressions in the clay, which sometimes correspond to the tokens inside.

The purpose of a bulla was most probably to guarantee the accuracy and authenticity of stored tokens in commercial transactions. Tokens kept on a string or in a bag could be tampered with; fraud was much less easy where the tokens were sealed away. If goods were being despatched, a sealed bulla might have acted as a bill of lading. In the event of a dispute, the bulla could be broken open and the contents checked against the merchandise.

By marking the outside of the clay, it would have been possible to check the contents without having to break the bulla, though of course such impressions would not have been as secure from tampering. But the evidence here is ambiguous. One would expect the number of exterior impressions to match the number of tokens. In some cases this is so, but not always. One might also expect a match between the shapes of the impressions and the shapes of the tokens. (Presumably, after the bulla was sealed, the impressions would be made with other tokens exactly like those hidden inside.) In fact, the correlation is patchy.

Some scholars, led by Denise Schmandt-Besserat, think that these exterior marks on bullae were a step towards the marking of clay tablets with more complex signs, and the consequent emergence of writing. While their theory is reasonable, it seems over-complicated. Why should a sign scratched in a tablet be considered a more advanced idea than an impression on a clay ball or, for that matter, than a clay token itself? If anything, the modelling of an engraved token seems to be more advanced than the scratching of a sign. Compare the invention of coins, which postdated scratch marks and notches on a tally stick. (There are notched Ice Age bones that may be lunar calendars.) Furthermore, tokens and bullae continued to be made long after the emergence of cuneiform writing. Rather than giving rise to the idea of full writing, as suggested, tokens and bullae probably acted as supplements to writing, like tallies. In other words, they did not precede writing, but rather accompanied its development.

Pictograms

So how did writing begin? Until the Enlightenment in the 18th century, the favoured explanation was divine invention, as in the story of Thoth told by Socrates. Today many, probably most, scholars accept that the earliest writing evolved from accountancy – not via the clay tokens but nonetheless as a result of commercial requirements.

The earliest writings from Mesopotamia, fired clay tablets dating from around 3300 BC, are all accounting records, while the earliest evidence for writing in Egypt, dating from around 3200 BC, is to be found in the symbols on tags made of bone and ivory used for the identification and counting of grave goods. (Neither date is certain, and some Egyptologists claim a slightly earlier date for Egyptian writing.) The earliest writing from Europe, the Linear A and Linear B clay tablets from Crete/mainland Greece belonging to the mid-2nd millennium BC, are account records. Although it is puzzling that in China, India, and Meso-America accountancy is little in evidence in the earliest writing, the reason may simply be that such accounts have not survived. Commercial record keeping in these early civilizations may have been on perishable materials like bamboo, bark, or animal skin. Such materials decayed and disappeared, unlike those in Mesopotamia, Egypt, and Crete. Even clay tablets in many cases have endured only because they were accidentally baked and hardened during the incineration of palace archives.

In other words, some time in the late 4th millennium BC, in the cities of Sumer in Mesopotamia – the 'cradle of civilization' between the rivers Tigris and Euphrates – an expanding economy compelled the creation of writing. The complexity of trade and administration reached a point where it outstripped the power of memory among the governing elite. To record transactions in a dependable, permanent form became essential to government and commerce. Administrators and merchants could then say the Sumerian equivalent of 'I shall put this in writing' and 'Can I have this in writing?'

Some scholars believe that a conscious search for a solution to this problem by an unknown Sumerian individual in the city of Uruk (biblical Erech), circa 3300 BC, produced writing. Others posit that writing was the work of a group, presumably of clever administrators and merchants. Still others think it was not an invention at all, but an accidental discovery. Many regard it as the result of evolution over a long period, rather than a flash of inspiration. These are all reasonable hypotheses, given the severely limited evidence, and we shall probably never know which of them is actually correct.

What is virtually certain, though, is that the first written symbols began life as pictures. Many of the earliest signs from Mesopotamia, Egypt, and China are easily recognizable pictograms. They depict creatures such as fish, birds, and pigs, plants such as barley and date-palms, parts of the body such as hands and heads, objects like baskets and pots, and natural scenes like the sun, moon, mountains, and rivers.

Some of the early pictograms represent abstract concepts, too. Thus a drawing of a leg and foot may stand not only for 'leg and foot' but also for the concept of 'walk' or 'stand', and a head with a bowl near its mouth may stand for 'eat'. In such cases, the symbolism is universally comprehensible, yet this is not generally true of pictograms.

In the first place, a picture can become so stylized and simplified that it is no longer recognizable as a pictogram. This change happened during the development of Mesopotamian pictograms

2. These pictograms from Mesopotamia appear on Sumerian clay tablets, dating from c. 3000 BC. They have the following meanings:
top row: hand/day/cow/eat/pot/date-palm
middle row: pig/orchard/bird/reed/donkey/ox
bottom row: head/walk, stand/fish/barley/well/water

into certain signs of the cuneiform script and the later development of Chinese pictograms into elements of the character script. Although Egyptian hieroglyphic resisted the trend towards abstraction and remained clearly pictographic, it gave birth to a second, more abstract, administrative script known as hieratic, and much later to a third administrative script, demotic (written on the Rosetta Stone), where any resemblance to hieroglyphic is difficult to detect.

Second, at what point on a scale of increasing abstraction and association of ideas does the meaning of a pictogram fall? A standing male stick figure could mean, for example, anything from one individual to the totality of mankind; it could also symbolize 'stand', 'wait', 'alone', 'lonely', or indeed 'Men's WC'. Similarly, the Sumerian symbol for 'barley' could just as well mean any other kind of grain-producing plant, or indeed any plant. The situation with pictograms is somewhat similar to that of children learning to talk. Having learnt that the family dog is called 'dog', they may over-extend the word to other animals they see, such as cats – or they may use the word too narrowly, applying it only to one particular dog, their family dog.

The very earliest Sumerian tablets from Uruk consist of pictograms or quasi-pictograms and numerals. They concern calculations. Although we cannot be sure of the tablets' meaning in every detail, we can sometimes follow a calculation, as described in the seminal study *Archaic Bookkeeping: Writing and Techniques of Economic Administration in the Ancient Near East* written by a multidisciplinary team of scholars, Hans Nissen, Peter Damerow, and Robert Englund. (The title may not sound very inviting, but in fact the book can be as intellectually intriguing as a detective story.)

The Sumerian numerals were impressed in the clay tablet in ways that remained the same for many centuries, as the cuneiform script developed during the 3rd millennium BC. The round end of a reed stylus was either pressed vertically into the soft clay to make a circular hole, or it was pressed at an angle to make a fingernail-shaped depression – or a combination of both impressions, superimposed, was used to express a larger numeral. It is possible that the particular shapes created by the stylus developed out of the impressions made in the clay bullae. But it is equally possible that they were developed specially for use on the clay tablets.

The tablet shown on page 12 records a transaction in barley. The pictogram for barley appears twice, very plainly. The numerals at the top record the quantity of barley. The three fingernail-shaped depressions on the far left, each with a circular hole in it, write the biggest unit, corresponding to 43,200 litres, hence they total three times 43,200, which equals 129,600 litres. The grand total of all twelve numerals represents about 135,000 litres. Immediately beneath them on the left are the signs for the accounting period,

3. This early cuneiform clay tablet, from ancient Uruk in today's Iraq, dates from the late 4th millennium BC. It records a transaction involving barley. See the text for a fuller explanation

37 months; if you look carefully, you can see three circular holes standing for 30 and 7 small depressions enclosed in the sign for 'month'. Immediately beneath this 'month' sign are two signs for the name of the responsible official or the name of an institution/office – a sort of Sumerian signature. On the basis of the two signs' resemblance to later cuneiform signs of known phonetic value, the official's name may have been 'Kushim'. Some other signs in the bottom right-hand corner are less clear in meaning, but may refer to the function of the document and the use of the barley. Given the very large amount of barley and the long accounting period (some three years), the tablet appears to be a summary of a 'balance sheet'.

In Egypt, the oldest group of inscribed artefacts – discovered only in the late 1980s – comes from a royal tomb known as U-j at Abydos, predating the dynastic period that began in 3100 BC. Some are ceramic jars, more than a hundred of them, bearing large single or paired signs on their walls. However the second type of artefact, the more intriguing of the two, consists of nearly 200 small bone and ivory tags just over one-and-a-quarter centimetres in height on average, drilled in one corner, which look as if they were once attached to bales of cloth or other valuable grave goods that have vanished with tomb robbers. Inscribed on the tags are numerals – in groups of up to twelve single digits, plus the sign for 100 and for 100 + 1 – and pictographic signs, although puzzlingly the numerals and the pictograms hardly occur together on the same tag. At least some of the pictograms, but certainly not the majority, strongly resemble later hieroglyphic signs, in particular some birds, a stretch of water, and possibly a cobra.

According to the tags' excavator, the signs are precursors of the hieroglyphs. They show the existence of a writing system that would give rise to the familiar hieroglyphs within a few hundred years, moreover a system inspired by economics, as with the inventories written on the Uruk clay tablets. However this

4. These bone tags from tomb U-j at Abydos, dating from c. 3200 BC, are the oldest group of inscribed artefacts so far known in Egypt. Some scholars believe that the pictograms on the tags were precursors of the later hieroglyphic writing system, which appeared some time between 3100 and 3000 BC

conclusion is doubtful. While the element of accountancy in the tags is undeniable, the existence of a writing system is unproven, and the connection with the hieroglyphs is speculative. At present, there is simply no way to be sure of the precise usage and meaning of this limited repertoire of primitive signs, or of how they may have been connected with the later hieroglyphs; and there is nothing in the signs that requires a phonetic reading based on the Egyptian language. Unless considerably more material is discovered by archaeologists, there is unlikely to be a consensus about the significance of the U-j inscriptions, apart from the fact that they predate all other writing found in Egypt.

The origin of full writing

The writing on the Uruk tablet and the U-j bone tags is not full writing, but rather a developed form of proto-writing. So far as we know, none of its signs expresses the phonetic values of the Sumerian or Egyptian language spoken in the late 4th millennium, unlike the signs of the cuneiform and hieroglyphic scripts in the subsequent millennium – with the possible exception of the signs that may read 'Kushim'. The numerals and the pictograms, such as those showing barley and birds, may be read in any language, not only Sumerian or Egyptian.

Some time after the creation of these very early pieces of writing and before the appearance of the cuneiform and hieroglyphic scripts, which has been dated to 3100–3000 BC, there was a breakthrough into full writing. The concept of the rebus was invented (we do not know how). It is the rebus principle that permits words to be written in terms of their constituent parts that cannot be depicted pictographically. The rebus – which comes from a Latin word meaning 'by things' – permits the parts of any spoken word, including abstract concepts, to be written in signs. With the rebus principle, sounds could be made visible in a systematic way, and abstract concepts symbolized.

Rebuses are familiar today from puzzle-picture writing, and also to some extent from electronic text messaging. For instance, Lewis Carroll, author of *Alice's Adventures in Wonderland*, liked to write rebus letters to child friends. One of his puzzle-picture letters has little pictures of a deer for 'dear', an eye for 'I', and a hand for 'and'. My surname, Robinson, could be written as a rebus using a picture of a robin followed by a picture of the sun; and my first name, Andrew, might (at a stretch) be written as a picture of a hand, standing for 'and', followed by a pencil making a drawing, standing for 'drew'. Still staying with English examples, a picture of a bee with a picture of a tray might stand for 'betray', while a picture of a bee with a figure 4 might represent 'before'.

Ancient rebuses include a Sumerian accounting tablet from about 3000 BC. The symbol in its top left-hand corner is a pictogram representing the Sumerian word for 'reed', pronounced *gi*. Yet on this tablet the sign does not mean 'reed' but is a rebus for 'reimburse', an abstract concept also pronounced *gi* in Sumerian. 'Reed' and 'reimburse' are homophonous – they have the same sound – in Sumerian, like 'son' and 'sun' in English. In Egyptian hieroglyphs, which are full of rebuses, the 'sun' pictogram, ⊙, pronounced *r(a)* or *r(e)*, stands for both the sun god Ra and the first symbol in the hieroglyphic spelling of the pharaoh known as Ramesses (in his ancient Greek spelling). There is even a statue of Ramesses II in which the entire image is a rebus. It makes visual sense as a boy with a solar disc on his head and in his hand a reed plant, the heraldic symbol of Upper Egypt. But it can also be read phonetically as three hieroglyphs – sun, child, and reed – pronounced *r(a)*, *ms* and *sw*: the Egyptian spelling of Ramesses.

There is obviously more to full writing than pictograms and rebuses. But it was this combination of ideas, whether invented, stumbled upon, or gradually developed in the late 4th millennium BC, which allowed writing systems to begin to convey 'any and all thought' that was expressible in spoken words.

Chapter 2

Development and diffusion of writing

Once writing of the full kind was invented, accidentally discovered, or evolved – take your pick – in Mesopotamia, or perhaps in nearby Egypt, did it then diffuse from there throughout the globe: eastwards to India, China, and Japan, westwards to Europe and to Meso-America? Or was writing independently invented in each of the world's earliest civilizations, without external influence? Despite much debate, this interesting conundrum has yet to be resolved. There are arguments to support both a single origin and multiple origins.

On present archaeological evidence, full writing appeared in Mesopotamia and Egypt around the same time, in the century or so before 3000 BC. It is probable that it started slightly earlier in Mesopotamia, given the date of the earliest proto-writing on clay tablets from Uruk, circa 3300 BC, and the much longer history of urban development in Mesopotamia compared to the Nile Valley of Egypt. However we cannot be sure about the date of the earliest known Egyptian historical inscription, a monumental slate palette of King Narmer, on which his name is written in two hieroglyphs showing a catfish and a chisel. Narmer's date is insecure, but probably falls in the period 3150 to 3050 BC. (Tomb U-j at Abydos predates Narmer's palette, but did not contain any indisputably hieroglyphic inscriptions.)

In India, writing dates from about 2500 BC, with the appearance of complex, exquisitely inscribed signs on seal stones in the cities of the Indus Valley civilization, which was discovered in the 1920s. However the Indus Valley script is undeciphered, so we do not know if the seal stones are full writing or proto-writing. Most scholars assume full writing, given the sophistication of the civilization and the seal stones, but as yet there is no proof. Perplexingly, the earliest unequivocal full writing in India is a completely different script, the Brahmi script, which dates from only 250 BC, leaving a gap without writing of perhaps a millennium and a half after the disappearance of the Indus script around 1800 BC.

In China, full writing first appears on the so-called 'oracle bones' of the Shang civilization, found about a century ago at Anyang in north China, dated to 1200 BC. Many of their signs bear an undoubted resemblance to modern Chinese characters, and it is a fairly straightforward task for scholars to read the oracle bones in Chinese. However, there are much older signs on the pottery of the Yangshao culture, dating from 5000 to 4000 BC, which may conceivably be precursors of an older form of full Chinese writing, still to be discovered; many areas of China have yet to be archaeologically excavated.

In Europe, the oldest full writing is the Linear A script found in Crete in 1900 on Minoan tablets. Linear A dates from about 1750 BC. Although it is undeciphered, its signs closely resemble the somewhat younger, deciphered Linear B script, which is known to be full writing; Linear B was used to write an archaic form of the Greek language.

In Meso-America, the earliest script is the Olmec script, belonging to the artistically sophisticated Olmec civilization that existed in the Veracruz region on the Gulf of Mexico. The first convincing sample of this script was found only in the late 1990s. It has been dated to about 900 BC, more than a millennium before the

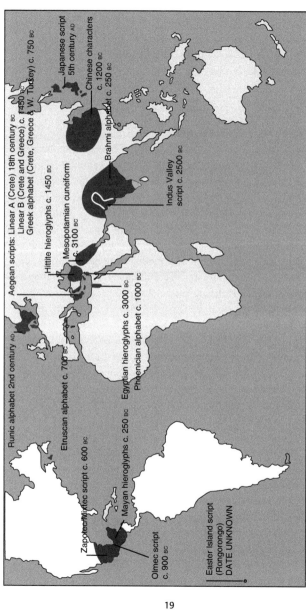

Aegean scripts: Linear A (Crete) 18th century BC
Linear B (Crete and Greece) c. 1450 BC
Greek alphabet (Crete, Greece & W. Turkey) c. 750 BC

Japanese script 5th century AD

Chinese characters c. 1200 BC

Brahmi alphabet c. 250 BC

Indus Valley script c. 2500 BC

Hittite hieroglyphs c. 1450 BC

Mesopotamian cuneiform c. 3100 BC

Runic alphabet 2nd century AD

Etruscan alphabet c. 700 BC

Egyptian hieroglyphs c. 3000 BC

Phoenician alphabet c. 1000 BC

Zapotec/Mixtec script c. 600 BC

Mayan hieroglyphs c. 250 BC

Olmec script c. 900 BC

Easter Island script (Rongorongo) DATE UNKNOWN

5. The early civilizations of Mesopotamia, Egypt, India, Europe, China, and Meso-America all produced writing, as shown in this map. The dates are approximate and in a few cases controversial

19

appearance of the hieroglyphic script of the Maya in the Yucatan region. Although the Olmec sample is very small, and the script is undeciphered, there is reason to believe that it may be full writing – the first in the Americas.

Single origin versus multiple origins

Thus we have the following approximate dates of origin for full writing: Mesopotamia 3100 BC, Egypt 3100–3000 BC, India 2500 BC, Crete 1750 BC, China 1200 BC, Meso-America 900 BC. On the basis of this chronology, it seems logical to assume that the idea of writing diffused gradually from Mesopotamia to other cultures. The concept of combining pictograms with the rebus principle could have been borrowed, and used to create a new set of signs suitable for the language spoken by the borrowers. Script borrowing with varying degrees of modification of the borrowed signs has occurred in numerous periods and regions throughout history. For example, the Etruscans of northern Italy borrowed their basic alphabet from the Greeks in the 8th century BC and used it to write the Etruscan language. The Japanese borrowed the character script of China to create their even more complex writing system during the 1st millennium AD. In the colonial period of the 19th and 20th centuries, the Roman alphabet was borrowed and modified to write many hitherto unwritten languages throughout the world.

Looking east, China could surely have borrowed the idea of writing from Mesopotamia during the 3rd/2nd millennium BC or after via the Central Asian cultures of the Silk Route, and gone on to develop the unique set of Chinese characters. For comparison, the idea of printing took 600 or 700 years to reach Europe from China, and the idea of paper, which was invented in China in the early 2nd century AD or before, took even longer to spread via the Silk Route to 8th-century Baghdad and thereby reach Europe in the 11th century. On the Indian subcontinent, the Indus Valley dwellers unquestionably had trading contacts with Mesopotamia via the

Persian Gulf. Cuneiform inscriptions give the Mesopotamian name Meluhha for what appears to be the Indus Valley, and Indus seals have been excavated in Mesopotamia. There was plenty of opportunity for the Indus civilization to have borrowed the idea of writing from the Middle East.

Looking west, Minoan Crete is known to have had contact with the Egyptian and maybe the Anatolian civilizations bordering the Mediterranean, so it is possible to imagine the invention of a Minoan script stimulated by hieroglyphs or perhaps cuneiform.

6. This broken stone seal, with undeciphered signs along the top that appear to be writing, is from the Indus Valley civilization, dating from the second half of the 3rd millennium BC. Its excavator dubbed it 'Proto-Shiva', because the 'yogic' figure wearing a horned headdress reminded him of the Hindu god Shiva. There is, however, no evidence at all for this identification

Indeed the earliest form of Minoan proto-writing, seal pictograms predating Linear A, bears some passing resemblance to Egyptian hieroglyphs. Later, during the early 1st millennium BC, the Greeks undoubtedly borrowed their alphabetic signs from the script of the Phoenicians, who traded throughout the Mediterranean. As for Meso-America, the idea of writing could in theory have been transmitted across the Atlantic Ocean at some time during the two millennia that elapsed between its invention in the Old World and its appearance in the New. This possibility certainly seems far-fetched, but it is not inconceivable given the undoubted long eastward sea voyages across the Pacific Ocean in prehistoric times that populated Polynesia, as far as remote Easter Island, which was probably settled from the Marquesas Islands, 4000 kilometres away, during the early centuries AD.

On the other hand, it must be said that there is no evidence for any such borrowings from Mesopotamia by writers in China, the Indus Valley, Crete, or Meso-America. Moreover the signs of the scripts from these regions are extraordinarily unlike each other – almost as dissimilar as cuneiform is from Egyptian hieroglyphic. Even in the case of the much more proximate civilizations of Mesopotamia and Egypt, there is no definite evidence, only informed speculation. We know, for instance, that as early as 3500 BC, the blue gemstone lapis lazuli had reached Egypt, presumably from Afghanistan, its nearest and most important source, which is much further away from Egypt than Sumer. But at present all we can say with confidence is that the signs on the clay tablets of Uruk and on the bone tags of tomb U-j at Abydos appear to have evolved at around the same time independently of each other, in order to manage the economies of their respective cultures.

As a result, scholars of writing are divided on the issue of origins. During much of the 20th century, 'stimulus diffusion' of writing from Mesopotamia across the world was the fashion. Today, with the colonial empires gone, the fashion is more for independent invention. The optimist, or at any rate the anti-imperialist, will prefer to emphasize the intelligence and inventiveness of human societies; the pessimist, who takes a more conservative view of history, will tend to assume that humans prefer to copy what already exists, as faithfully as they can, restricting their innovations to cases of absolute necessity. 'Many scholars working on early writing systems today would be happy with the proposition that Sumerian, Egyptian, Chinese, and Mayan were all created in response to local needs and without stimulus by pre-existing writing systems from elsewhere', writes the Assyriologist Jerrold Cooper in a recent collection of articles entitled *The First Writing*.

Having looked at the origins of the earliest scripts, we shall now glance at how each developed over the course of its existence, beginning with the oldest script, cuneiform.

Cuneiform

Cuneiform writing arose out of the 'proto-cuneiform' pictograms pressed into clay tablets at Uruk with the wedge-shaped end of a reed stylus. (The numerals, by contrast, were made with the other, round end of the stylus.) The term cuneiform derives from 'cuneus', the Latin word for 'wedge'. By about 2500 BC, the pictograms had become cuneiform signs in widespread use for writing the language of the Sumerians; later they developed into the script of the Babylonian, Assyrian, and Hittite empires; and in the Persian empire of Darius, around 500 BC, a new alphabetic cuneiform script was invented to write the Persian language, which is displayed in the ceremonial inscriptions of Persepolis, the capital of Darius's empire. The latest inscription in cuneiform, from Babylon, is dated AD 75. Thus, cuneiform was employed as a writing system for some 3000 years – considerably longer than today's Roman alphabet and almost as long as Egyptian hieroglyphs and Chinese characters.

Impressed in clay or inscribed on metal, ivory, glass, and wax, but rarely written in ink, so far as we know, cuneiform gave ancient

Mesopotamia a history. Rulers such as Sargon of Akkad, Hammurabi of Babylon, and the Assyrian king Sennacherib speak to us through their cuneiform inscriptions. Hammurabi, the sixth ruler of the first dynasty of Babylon, ruled an empire from 1792 to 1750 BC, and is most famous for his great law code, inscribed in Babylonian cuneiform on a diorite stela in the most important temple of Babylon and now kept at the Louvre Museum. The code contains 282 case laws dealing with the economy and with family, criminal, and civil law. One of them states: 'If a man has harboured in his house a fugitive slave or bondmaid belonging to the state or to a private citizen, and not brought him out at the summons of the public crier, the master of that house shall be slain.' The harshness was typical of the code, but it was surprisingly enlightened too on the subject of women and children, in an effort to protect them from arbitrary treatment, poverty, and neglect. It went far beyond tribal custom and recognized no blood feud, private retribution, or marriage by capture.

Yet there remain awkward gaps in the cuneiform record, for which no tablets or inscriptions have been discovered. We tend to assume that economic activity was low in these periods. In fact, the opposite may be true: they may have been periods of peace and prosperity. Unlike in times of strife and war – a favoured activity of the Babylonians, Assyrians, and Persians – perhaps during these gaps no one's cuneiform library was being burnt down, no invaluable clay-tablet archive being accidentally baked for posterity.

With the discovery from the mid-19th century onwards of large numbers of tablets from many periods of Mesopotamian history, and the steady decipherment of the cuneiform used to write languages such as Sumerian, Akkadian, Babylonian, Elamite, and Assyrian, the evolution of certain signs could be discerned by scholars. The early numerical tablets from Uruk were seen to give way initially to signs made of wedges that still resembled the pictographic symbols; these in turn became further abstracted; and by the time of the Assyrian empire in the 1st millennium, the signs bore almost no resemblance to their pictographic progenitors.

At some point in the later 3rd millennium or earlier part of the 2nd millennium BC, the evolving signs underwent a change of orientation. The pictograms on clay tablets became turned through 90 degrees, so that they lay on their backs. It was the same for the overall direction of the script (though it was still often partitioned into columns like a modern newspaper). Moreover, instead of being written from right to left, the script was now written from left to right. But stone monuments continued to be written in the orientation of the archaic script until the middle of the 2nd millennium. So, in order to read Hammurabi's law code, one must hold one's head down on one's right shoulder (turning the eyes through 90 degrees).

The date of this change is vague, and the reason for it is not clear. Some scholars have proposed that it came about because right-to-left writing tended to obliterate signs through smudging of the clay by the right hand. In fact, with good quality clay, this does not occur. A more likely reason is that the scribes found the new orientation more convenient to the way they held their tablet and stylus. Experiments with a tablet and stylus suggest this. In the words of the cuneiformist Marvin Powell, 'there must have been from the beginning a strong tendency to *write* the tablet at an angle rather different from that at which it was read.'

Egyptian hieroglyphs

Unlike in cuneiform, pictography remained an integral part of Egyptian hieroglyphic, from its beginnings before 3000 BC to its latest inscription written in the gate of Hadrian on the island of Philae near Aswan in AD 394. However, soon after 2700 BC, the cursive ('joined-up') hieratic script developed from hieroglyphic, and continued in parallel with it. Both wrote the same language, but while hieroglyphic was used essentially for monumental, religious, and funerary purposes, on stone and papyri, the more rapidly written hieratic was employed mainly for administrative and business purposes (confusingly, given its sacred-sounding name), on papyri. Then, after about 650 BC, a third script, demotic, developed from hieratic. Demotic took over the role of hieratic in administration and commerce, while hieratic became a priestly script, as its name implies, used for religious and funerary matters. Demotic was also used, unlike hieratic, for monuments, such as the Rosetta Stone (196 BC). But it had nothing to do with the spreading of literacy 'to the people', as suggested by its name: 'demotic' derives from 'demotika', Greek for '[script] in common use' – unlike, of course, the monumental hieroglyphic.

Egyptian hieroglyphs were written and read both from right to left and from left to right. Always, whichever direction was chosen, the individual signs faced in such a way that the reader's eye passed over them from front to back. Thus, if one looks at a line of hieroglyphs and sees the signs (birds, humans, animals, etc.) facing to the right, then the direction of writing is from right to left – and vice versa. That said, the Egyptians usually wrote from right to left, unless there was a pressing reason to choose a particular direction. Reasons for choosing left to right included aesthetic appeal and symmetry, the showing of respect towards images of gods, kings, and others, and physical ease of reading.

A nice example is the so-called false door of Khut-en-Ptah – 'false' because the sculpted doorway is actually solid. In an Egyptian tomb, such doors marked the boundary between the closed and forbidden domain of the dead and a relatively accessible area where friends and relatives of the deceased could make prayers and offerings. The deceased Khut-en-Ptah is shown twice at the bottom to the left of the door, and twice to the right, in each case facing inwards. The columns of hieroglyphs directly above her images all face inwards too; those on the right are therefore mirror images of those on the left (though they are not in exactly the same order). The sculptor did, however, make one mistake, carving a sign showing a basket with a handle on one side the same way around on both left and right of the door, instead of remembering to reverse the handle on the right side, as in a mirror image.

The symmetry is pleasing, and also the natural way for a 'person' passing through the false door to view and read the hieroglyphs on either side: from right to left, to the left of the door, and from left to right, to the right of the door. The lines of hieroglyphs above the door are, by contrast, read naturally in only one direction, and so they are written from right to left.

The ancient Egyptians were obsessed with death and the afterlife. They had many versions of the Book of the Dead, which began life in the 16th century BC. This consisted of religious spells written in both hieroglyphic and hieratic on papyrus rolls with copious illustrations; stored in the tomb of the deceased, the Book of the Dead was thought to ensure happiness in the other world. The quality varied enormously, depending on the wealth of the individual named in the book: some books were specially commissioned with an individual choice of texts and beautiful illustrations, others were standard copies, without much artistry, in which a space had been left to add the buyer's name and titles. In one of the finer examples, dated to 1000–800 BC, belonging to a man named Pawiaenadja, the dead man is depicted pouring cool water on some offerings piled upon an altar before the god Osiris. His name appears in the last column of hieroglyphs above his head. It appears to mean 'the sacred barque of the boy'. The 'boy' is represented both phonetically and literally, by the hieroglyph depicting a child pointing its finger at its mouth, which faces to the left; the derived, similar-looking hieratic sign opposite the illustration shows the child facing to the right.

Linear A and B

In *The Odyssey*, Homer refers to Crete – 'lovely and fertile and ocean-rounded' – and its 90 cities, among them 'mighty Knossos'.

Its king was once Minos, 'who every ninth year took counsel with Zeus himself'. Some two and a half millennia after Homer, in 1900, the archaeologist Arthur Evans began to dig up and reconstruct the site of ancient Knossos in the northern part of central Crete. He discovered what he believed was the palace of King Minos, with its notorious labyrinth, home of the Minotaur. He also discovered two new scripts – the earliest writing in Europe.

'Linear Script of Class B' was the name Evans gave to the fairly primitive signs scratched on clay tablets that he discovered soon after he began to excavate. The 'Class B' label was to distinguish the signs from quite similar-looking but nevertheless distinct signs on archaeologically older tablets that Evans had labelled 'Linear Script of Class A'. Though found at Knossos with Linear B, most Linear A tablets came initially from another Minoan palace excavated (not by Evans) in southern Crete, at Haghia Triada.

The term 'Linear' was used not because the signs were written in sequence but because they consisted of lines inscribed on the flat surface of the clay, perhaps with a thorn or bronze point. They were a mixture of mainly abstract and numerical signs with some simple pictograms, for example 'man', 'horse', 'tripod', 'amphora', 'spear', 'chariot', and 'wheel'. This writing was quite different from the three-dimensional, engraved images of a third, primarily pictographic Cretan script, found chiefly on seal stones and only in the eastern part of the island, which Evans dubbed 'Hieroglyphic' but which actually did not much resemble Egyptian writing.

Linear A and Linear B tablets are uninspiring objects to the eye of the uninitiated, unlike Egyptian hieroglyphic inscriptions and many of the cuneiform inscriptions. They were basic bureaucratic palace records, accidentally preserved by fire, intended to last at most for a few years not for posterity. They remind us of how much of the writing from these early civilizations must have perished and returned to dust. Flat, smooth pieces of clay, their colour generally dull grey but sometimes like red brick (the result of greater oxidation when the tablet was burnt), their sizes vary from small sealings and labels little more than two-and-a-half centimetres across to heavy, page-shaped tablets designed to be held in a single hand, the largest Linear B tablet being as big as a fair-sized paperback.

According to the archaeological record available to Evans, the Cretan Hieroglyphic was the oldest of the three scripts, dating chiefly to 2100–1700 BC; Linear A belonged to the period 1750–1450 BC; while Linear B slightly post-dated Linear A. Evans therefore came to the conclusion that all three scripts wrote the same 'Minoan' language indigenous to Crete, and that Linear B had developed from Linear A, which in turn had probably developed from the older Hieroglyphic script – on the basis that the later Egyptian scripts such as hieratic and demotic were derived from Egyptian hieroglyphic and that all of them wrote one Egyptian language. This notion was consistent with the idea, prevalent in Evans's time, that writing systems always evolved from pictograms like the Cretan 'hieroglyphs' into comparatively abstract signs like the majority of the signs in Linear A and B.

Today this simple picture of Cretan script descent has been abandoned. Linear B was deciphered in the 1950s (after the death of Evans) and shown to write archaic Greek, not a new Minoan language. Linear A has been to some degree deciphered but appears to write an unknown language – only possibly Cretan in origin – so that we cannot really read it. The Hieroglyphic seal script remains almost wholly mysterious, and is generally regarded as proto-writing, not full writing as in Linear A and B. Furthermore, all three scripts have been found outside Crete, around the Aegean (even in Anatolia), and the spans of their dates are now seen to overlap. While Hieroglyphic remains certainly the oldest script, Linear A the next oldest, and Linear B the youngest, we know that Hieroglyphic coexisted for a while with Linear A, and so did Linear A with Linear B. Scholars no longer postulate a straightforward line of descent purely within Crete: Linear A and

Linear B may be cousin scripts, rather than the first being the parent of the second.

The latest Linear B inscriptions, found in the destroyed palace of ancient Pylos on the Greek mainland, date from about 1200 BC. This was the beginning of a so-called Dark Age of apparent illiteracy, which included the Trojan War described by Homer in *The Iliad*. When writing re-emerged in Greece in the 8th century after a gap of some 400 years, it was in the form of the Greek alphabet, entirely unrelated to Linear B.

Chinese characters

Claims for the great antiquity of Chinese characters have long been made, but only in 1899 was reliable early Chinese writing discovered. It was in the form of the so-called oracle bones. For many years before this, traditional Chinese medicine shops in Beijing had sold 'dragon bones', which were in fact old turtle shells and ox scapulae churned up by farmers' ploughs in a village near the town of Anyang in northern Henan province. Signs were frequently found scratched on the surface of these objects; they were usually hacked off with a spade by the farmers before the bones were sold, as being inappropriate to dragon bones. The signs were, however, of great interest to two scholars in Beijing, Wang Yirong and Liu E, who recognized that some of the signs were similar to the characters on early bronze inscriptions. They bought up all of the inscribed shell and bone fragments they could find in the medicine shops of the capital and published rubbings of the inscriptions.

The 'dragon bones' turned out to be the earliest known Chinese writing. They are records of divinations by the twelve later kings of the Shang dynasty, who ruled from about 1400–1200 BC. When heated, prepared turtle shells and ox scapulae cracked in special ways, and the cracks were read by diviners. A fairly typical inscription from the reign of Wu Ding, about childbirth, translates as follows: 'The king, reading the cracks, said: "If it be a 'ding' day childbearing, it will be good. If it be a 'geng' day childbearing, it will be extremely auspicious." The verification reads: 'On the thirty-first day, "jia-yin" (day 51), she gave birth. It was not good. It was a girl.'

A literate Chinese person, untutored in the ancient script, would probably find much of an oracle bone inscription incomprehensible at first glance, but after a little study the connections would begin to emerge. Yet many of the Shang signs have no modern descendants, just as many modern Chinese characters have no Shang ancestors. Of the 4,500 Shang signs distinguished to date, some 1,000 have been identified, and in many cases their evolution has been traced through three millennia to a modern character.

Some of these modern characters are pictographic in origin, based on Shang pictograms of a woman, a mouth, a mountain, a river, or a tree, for example. But the proportion of pictograms is much less than often suggested. No one doubts that pictography was important in the origins of Chinese characters, but it was certainly *not* the overriding principle in the formation of the early signs. Modern Chinese characters cannot be said to be basically pictographic in origin; and even those that once were definitely pictographic may show imperceptible iconicity.

The changes in style of writing a given character generally reflect periods in Chinese history. The Shang dynasty was followed by the long-lasting Zhou dynasty, in which the Great Seal script flourished. Politically and administratively, however, this was a long period of disunity. Characters were created by writers living in different historical periods and speaking different dialects: the effect was greatly to complicate the use of phoneticism in the Chinese script. With the establishment of the unified empire of Qin in 221 BC, a spelling reform was introduced along with a simplified Small Seal script. The latter remained in use until the

7. The Chinese characters in oracle bone inscriptions from the Shang civilization, dating from 1200 BC, in many cases closely resemble modern Chinese characters. They are records of royal divinations

Shang	Great Seal	Small Seal	Scribal	Regular	Simplified

'come'

'horse'

8. The evolution of two Chinese characters over some 3,000 years shows how those characters that were originally pictographic became more abstract with time. See the text for a fuller explanation

1950s, when the Communist rulers of China introduced the present, still-controversial Simplified script.

The illustration shows the evolution of two characters from Shang to Simplified script. Both are pictographic but in different ways: the first character, 'lái', means 'come' and derives rebus-wise from the homophonous word for 'wheat' (which in its archaic form it depicts); the second character, 'mǎ', means 'horse'. The Great Seal script was the style of the Zhou dynasty (c. 1028–221 BC), the Small Seal script the style of the Qin dynasty (221–206 BC), and the Scribal and Regular scripts the styles of the Han dynasty (206 BC–AD 220).

Over 3,000 years and more, the number of Chinese characters increased dramatically from the 4,500 found in the Shang period. In the Han dynasty, there were almost 10,000, despite the reform of the Qin dynasty; by the 12th century, there were 23,000; and by the 18th century, there were almost 49,000 characters – many of them, to be sure, variants and obsolete forms. Of these, 2,400 suffice to read 99 per cent of today's texts. The overall appearance of the characters changed considerably over time, and many individual characters suffered attrition in form, all of which greatly muddled the picture of how particular characters have come to have the meanings they have, based on their constituent parts.

Nevertheless, the basic principles on which Chinese characters have been constructed have remained unchanged.

Meso-American writing

The Olmec civilization appeared around 1200 BC on the coast of the Gulf of Mexico and flourished until 400 BC: the first developed civilization in Meso-America. Olmec motifs on pottery and other media, and a few signs that looked as if they might be glyphs, had been noted by archaeologists for some years; but they had found no inscription that would suggest the existence of full writing. It seemed that the Olmecs, like the much later Incas, had no writing.

Then in 1999, road builders quarrying fill from an ancient mound at Cascajal in the Isthmus of Tehuantepec spotted a substantially inscribed stone block, along with Olmec pottery fragments and figurines. If the block is of the same age as the accompanying artefacts, then it dates from 900 BC. However, the inscription consists of only 62 signs, some of which are repeated – far too few for a decipherment, especially as nothing certain is known of the Olmec spoken language. Some scholars dispute whether the inscription qualifies as full writing, but the majority think it does. Seven of them, writing in the journal *Science* in 2006–7 after intensive study of the block, concluded that it is 'the oldest example of writing in the New World and among the most important finds ever made in Meso-America.'

The Olmec legacy was highly influential in Meso-America, especially in the realm of religion. But a relationship between Olmec writing and subsequent Meso-American writing systems, though possible, is unclear. More than a dozen of these later scripts have been distinguished by scholars. The most significant of them in the aftermath of the Olmec civilization are: the Zapotec script, dating from perhaps as early as 600 BC but probably later; the Isthmian script (also known as the epi-Olmec script, since it comes from the same region as the Olmec civilization), dating from the

2nd century AD; and – the most important script of all – Mayan glyphs. Although the earliest Mayan inscription dates from the 3rd century AD, it is almost inconceivable that such a complex script would not have had a period of gestation and development during the preceding few centuries. From various lines of evidence, it seems that the Maya took the idea of writing – though not their particular signs – from the earlier scripts of Meso-America.

Chapter 3
Disappearance of scripts

The birth and growth of writing have been the focus of more study than the death of scripts. Yet much more is known about script death than about script birth. This knowledge shows that no single theory can encompass why scripts flourish or vanish. Commerce, culture, language, politics, prestige, religion, and technology, in varying combinations, are all implicated in the survival and disappearance of scripts. 'Their loss may be just as revealing as their first appearance', comments the Egyptologist John Baines in a recent collection of articles entitled *The Disappearance of Writing Systems*.

In antiquity, a seismic shift in political power and cultural prestige in Egypt caused the decline of hieroglyphic and demotic and the adoption of a new writing system. Egypt was conquered in 332 BC by Alexander the Great, who founded Alexandria, and was then ruled by the Greek-speaking Ptolemy dynasty, which used an alphabet; hence the Greek alphabet inscribed on the Rosetta Stone, along with hieroglyphic and demotic. However, the Egyptian scripts were not abolished. Instead, hieroglyphic was slowly marginalized by a flux of politics, language, script, and religion. After the death of Cleopatra, the last Ptolemaic ruler, in 30 BC, Egypt became a province of the Roman empire, which wrote in the Roman script; the spread of Christianity in Egypt gave rise to the Coptic church, which wrote in the Coptic alphabet; and in the 7th century AD, Egypt was conquered by Arabs who wrote in the Arabic script of Islam. All these political, linguistic, religious, and cultural changes together fossilized the hieroglyphs.

In modern times, an equally far-reaching change in politics and cultural prestige was again responsible for a major change in script in Turkey. But here the existing script was summarily abolished, rather than gradually eclipsed. In 1928, the founder of the secular Turkish state, Kemal Atatürk, banned the Arabic script that had been used during the Ottoman empire for writing the Turkish language. For government and education, Atatürk substituted a modified form of the Roman alphabet, as part of his drive to modernize Turkey, bring its culture closer to Europe, and distance it from the neighbouring Islamic world. Today, very few Turks can read Ottoman Turkish in Arabic script, and fairly soon this combination of language and script will cease to be understood, except by scholars. In centuries to come, it might even need to be deciphered, like Egyptian hieroglyphic.

In 20th-century China, by contrast, when another strong leader, Mao Zedong, proposed to romanize the Chinese script, so as to spread education to the masses and modernize the nation, he was forced by conservative literati to accept a limited and mixed reform. Mao first made his proposal in the 1930s, before the foundation of the People's Republic in 1949. In 1955, the Communist government introduced the Simplified character script, and in 1958 a parallel romanized phonetic system, Pinyin (meaning 'spell-sound'). This compromise happened because of the extraordinary prestige attached to the classical Chinese script, as a result of its antiquity going back to the Shang civilization, its long literary heritage, and its uniquely artistic tradition of calligraphy; indeed Mao himself was considered a good calligrapher. Despite the evident difficulties of writing the Chinese characters – for native-speaking writers as well as outsiders – not to speak of the challenge of computerizing them, the character script is unlikely to disappear any time soon, whether in China or in Japan. In Korea, however, Chinese characters have gradually given way to the Hangul alphabet invented by King Sejong and his scholars in the 1440s. Banned during the Japanese occupation of Korea from 1910 to 1945, since then Hangul has been universally accepted as Korea's national script, although Chinese characters (known as 'hanja') are still taught in schools in both North and South Korea.

With the exception of the Chinese characters, the scripts of all the major early civilizations – Mesopotamian cuneiform, Egyptian hieroglyphs, the Indus script, Linear A and B, Meso-American glyphs – eventually disappeared from use, as we know. Subsequently, there have been many other deaths of scripts, of which the following are especially important.

The Phoenician script of the Mediterranean area, immensely influential during the 1st millennium BC, which gave rise to the Greek alphabet, disappeared in the 1st century BC, after the Romans destroyed the Phoenician capital at Carthage in 146 BC. The Etruscan alphabet of northern Italy, which was originally borrowed from the Greek alphabet, gradually gave way to the Latin alphabet with the rise of Rome in the final centuries BC. The Kharosthi script of northwestern India, first used by the emperor Ashoka along with the Brahmi script in the 3rd century BC, was abandoned with the fall of the Kushan empire in the 3rd century AD. The Aramaic script of the Middle East, used by many peoples and empires in the 1st millennium BC, including the writers of the Dead Sea Scrolls, gave way to the Arabic script with the rise of Islam in the 7th century. The Meroitic hieroglyphs of Nubia in Sudan, script of the kingdom of Kush centred on the city of Meroe, which used signs based on the Egyptian hieroglyphs, disappeared around the 4th century AD with the disintegration of Kush. The 9th-century Glagolitic script, the first alphabet of any Slavonic language, used to translate the Bible into Old Bulgarian, was replaced in the 12th century by Cyrillic, the script of the Orthodox church, today used in Russia. The Phags-pa script, an alphabet derived from Tibetan writing by a Tibetan sage known as Phags-pa Lama, was invented in 1269 at the behest of the Mongol emperor Kublai Khan in order to write Mongolian throughout his empire,

9. The Dead Sea Scrolls, religious and legal texts dating from the 1st century BC to 1st century AD, were found in caves in Palestine during the mid-20th century. They are written in Hebrew and in Aramaic, a language that was widely used throughout the Middle East for a millennium during the centuries before and after the birth of Christ – using the Old Hebrew script and the Jewish script, one of the offshoots of the Aramaic cursive script

which by then included China. But Kublai Khan's Chinese officials were recalcitrant (as happened with Mao Zedong's officials in the 1950s), and so were ordinary Chinese and Mongols. The Phags-pa script did not catch on; its latest known inscription is dated 1352. Less important, yet intriguing, is the death of the Rongorongo script of remote Easter Island in the mid-19th century, after perhaps less than a century's use, for reasons that are still not clear.

The Americas, Australia, the Pacific region, most of Europe, and much of Africa nowadays write in the Roman alphabet. Only the Arab world and the majority of Asian countries prefer non-Roman scripts (though South Asia in practice treats the alphabet used to write English as a universal script). It may seem as if the Roman alphabet has achieved an immortality denied to all earlier scripts. Yet on the evidence of past disappearances of scripts, the continued global dominance of the Roman alphabet cannot be taken for granted during the current millennium.

The decline of cuneiform

The final centuries of cuneiform, and its disappearance from use around the time of Christ, are complicated. For example, a seal of Darius I, the Persian king who reigned from 521 to 486 BC, inscribed in cuneiform in three languages – Old Persian, Babylonian, and Elamite – was discovered at Thebes, the principal city of Upper Egypt (modern Luxor). Scholars think the object may have belonged to an Egyptianized Persian noble. This makes sense because the Persians conquered Egypt in 525 BC and ruled the country as the 27th dynasty of pharaohs until 404 BC.

Darius's most famous inscription, regarded as the 'Rosetta Stone of cuneiform' for its role in the decipherment of cuneiform, is the giant one at Behistun. It is cut into a cliff more than 100 metres above the road in the Zagros Mountains of western Iran near the little town of Behistun (today's Bisitun). A central bas-relief shows

King Darius, beneath the hovering Zoroastrian god Ahura Mazda, lording it over a line of captive kings he defeated in 522–520 BC in order to assume the throne of the Persian empire. Around the relief are massive panels of cuneiform, incised in the rock in Old Persian, Babylonian, and Elamite. More than two millennia later, in the 1830s and 1840s, a daring British army officer with a passion for languages and decipherment, Henry Creswicke Rawlinson, was able to take papier-mâché casts of the Behistun inscription using ladders and a roped platform with the help of 'a wild Kurdish boy' who squeezed himself up a cleft in the cliff and drove wooden pegs into the rock.

Old Persian cuneiform was most likely invented on the orders of Darius specifically to write the Behistun inscription, since there appear to be no earlier inscriptions in this type of cuneiform. It is much simpler than the cuneiform used to write the languages of Mesopotamia, such as Babylonian and Sumerian. Old Persian employs a system consisting of 36 phonetic signs. Most of the signs have three or four wedges, with a maximum of five. Mesopotamian cuneiform scripts have hundreds of signs, with up to 20 wedges. It is not difficult to understand why the victorious Darius commanded the creation of a new script to write his own imperial language.

But why did Darius not write the whole inscription in Old Persian cuneiform? Why include parallel versions in two declining scripts, Babylonian and Elamite? And why is there no inscription in Aramaic, which had become the lingua franca of the Middle East by the middle of the 1st millennium BC and an important administrative script of the Persian empire?

The reason would appear to be that Babylonian and Elamite cuneiform enjoyed high prestige in Persian eyes, while Aramaic did not. Babylon was the heartland of cuneiform, with a written tradition going back to Hammurabi and before. Elam, the region of southwestern Iran adjacent to Mesopotamia with its ancient

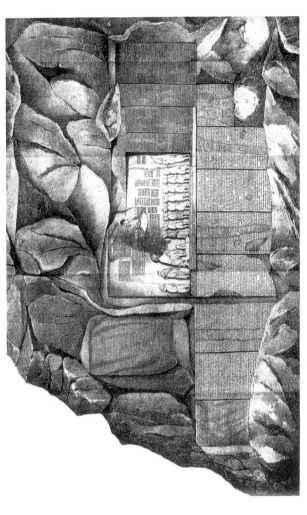

10. The rock at Behistun (Bisitun) in western Iran carries inscriptions in three cuneiform scripts, Old Persian, Babylonian, and Elamite, which greatly assisted the decipherment of cuneiform in the 19th century. The relief and inscriptions date from the reign of Darius, the Persian king (reigned 521–486 BC), who stands at the centre of the drawing

capital at Susa, had a tradition of writing even older than Babylonian, going back to the partially deciphered proto-Elamite tablets of about 3000 BC (though it is not clear whether these are full writing or not).

Both Babylonia and Elam were absorbed into the Persian empire in the 6th century BC. The increasing redundancy of cuneiform in Babylonia after the Persian conquest of Babylon in 539 BC offers a good case study of the multiple, often interdependent, causes of script obsolescence. There seem to have been three major causes of the gradual disappearance of Babylonian cuneiform: economic, linguistic, and administrative.

Economically, Babylon declined in importance when Alexander's alleged plan to make the city the capital of Asia, following his defeat of the Persian empire, failed to transpire after his death in 323 BC. The city was also bypassed by new desert trade routes from Asia to the Mediterranean, which opened up with the domestication of the camel as a pack animal. Seleucia, the city on the Tigris to the north of Babylon founded by one of Alexander's generals Seleucus Nicator, replaced Babylon as the leading city of Mesopotamia in the 3rd century BC and after. By the time of the Roman writer Pliny, around AD 50, Babylon had 'turned into a barren waste, exhausted by its proximity to Seleukeia'. The use of Babylon's cuneiform script therefore diminished in commercial transactions.

Linguistically, Babylonian cuneiform was disadvantaged as compared to alphabetic scripts. It was cumbersome, requiring many hundreds of signs – a mixture of syllables and logograms – and also a clay medium. Unlike the alphabets used to write Greek, Phoenician, and Aramaic, Babylonian cuneiform could not be written rapidly, cursively, and conveniently with a brush or pen and ink on papyrus and other lightweight materials. Nevertheless, the relationship between cuneiform and alphabets was not a straightforward one. Cuneiform was sometimes adapted to write alphabets. The earliest example is the cuneiform alphabet invented at Ugarit (modern Ras Shamra), on the north coast of Syria, in the 14th century BC. One of the Ugarit clay tablets shows a 30-sign 'abecedary' written in cuneiform – presumably to train apprentice scribes. Ugaritic cuneiform would have been gibberish to a Babylonian scribe.

Administratively, the Persian empire increasingly preferred the Aramaic script to cuneiform. Aramaic, originally a Semitic language of ancient Syria, grew in importance in the Middle East during the 1st millennium, as did its script. In due course it was the vernacular language of Jesus Christ and the Apostles. An Assyrian relief of the 8th century BC shows two scribes accompanying warriors, one of whom is writing in cuneiform, the other in Aramaic. In the Persian empire, Aramaic ran alongside cuneiform as an administrative script, and finally displaced it altogether.

At the end, sidelined by changes in economics, languages, and politics, Babylonian cuneiform's last refuge was astrology. According to the historian David Brown, scribes working in the collapsing temples of Babylon could still, as late as the 1st century AD, 'exploit a shrinking market for old-fashioned Babylonian astrology in cuneiform', even though they no longer wrote the script in an elegant hand.

The eclipse of Etruscan

The Etruscans were the principal intermediaries between the Greeks and non-Greeks, or 'barbarians', of the west. The Greeks first settled in Italy in about 775 BC, at Pithekoussai (modern Ischia). The Phoenicians were already established in western Sicily and Sardinia, and were commercially and politically allied with the Etruscans. Phoenician influence on the Etruscans was important, but Greek culture was paramount. Later the Etruscans transmitted Greek culture, including its alphabet, to their Latin-speaking neighbours, during the rise of Rome. Thus the Etruscan alphabet was the conduit by which the Roman alphabet established itself in Europe.

The Etruscans flourished as a separate people for several centuries until the 1st century BC, when they were effectively absorbed into the expanding Roman empire. Indeed, we owe a considerable amount of our knowledge of the Etruscans to Latin writings. It is clear that there was never an Etruscan empire, more a loose collection of individualistic, independent polities like the Greek city-states or the Tuscan cities of the Renaissance. What they had in common was their language and costumes that were distinct from other peoples in Italy and the Mediterranean – also the name by which they called themselves, 'rasna'.

The Romans treated the Etruscans with real respect, at one time sending their sons from Rome to the former centres of Etruscan power such as Caere (modern Cerveteri) where they probably learned the arts of divination, the 'disciplina etrusca', under the tutelage of an Etruscan 'haruspex'. It was a haruspex in Rome called Spurinna, a known Etruscan name, who warned Julius Caesar against the Ides of March; and even as late as AD 408 Etruscan haruspices recited prayers and incantations in vain to save Rome from being sacked by Alaric, king of the Goths. But although the Romans preserved much of Etruscan religious lore, which was useful to them, they showed little interest in Etruscan literature – preferring Greek literature, either in the original or in Latin translation – despite their borrowing of the Etruscan alphabet to write their own language.

Close study of Latin vocabulary shows that many words were originally loaned from Etruscan. Most were connected with luxurious living and higher culture – a tradition that endured in Tuscany in the Renaissance – including writing. Four examples to do with writing are the words 'elementum' (letter of the alphabet), 'litterae' (writing), 'stilus' (writing implement), and 'cera' (wax, as in wax tablets on which to take notes), which entered Latin by way of the Etruscan language.

Unfortunately, most of the Etruscan language is completely unknown. Latin has no relationship with it (loan words apart). Efforts have been made to link Etruscan with every European language, and languages such as Hebrew and Turkish, but it remains stubbornly isolated. This is particularly ironic, because the language was faithfully written in the Greek alphabet. We can easily read the 13,000 or so Etruscan inscriptions scattered over central Italy, but we cannot understand much of what they say – which is, in any case, often limited to the names of people and places, and dates. Our knowledge of Etruscan is comparable to what our knowledge of English would be if we had access only to English gravestones.

Etruscan-Latin bilingual inscriptions, of which there are about 30, though very short, have provided some useful information about Etruscan, especially about the relationship between the Etruscan cities and Rome in the 2nd and 1st centuries BC: the period when the Etruscans lost their independence and their language gradually died out. During this transition, both languages and both scripts were in use. But sometimes the Etruscan-language version and the Latin-language version were both written in Roman script.

An example of the latter is this bilingual marking the grave of two brothers Arnth and Vel, written entirely in Roman letters:

> **Etruscan**: 'Arnth Spedo Thocerual clan'
> [Arnth Spedo son of Thoceru]
> **Latin**: 'Vel Spedo Thoceronia natus'
> [Vel Spedo son of Thoceronia]

The equivalence of Etruscan 'clan' and Latin 'natus' (meaning 'son' in Latin), is obvious. Thoceru, the Etruscan name of the mother, becomes Thoceronia in the Latin inscription. However the family name Spedo is the same in both epitaphs, even though its Etruscan

11. The Tabula Cortonensis, dating from the 3rd or 2nd century BC, is the third-longest Etruscan inscription. Found in the area of Cortona, in central Italy, in the 1990s, it is made of bronze and inscribed on both sides. (Side A is shown here.) The Etruscan alphabet is read from right to left, and is based on the Greek alphabet. It is therefore a simple matter for scholars to read the script, but since the Etruscan language

(*cont. overpage*)

original was probably Spitu – known from other Etruscan inscriptions, whereas Spedo is unknown in Latin. Thus one brother, Arnth, the more conservative, records his name in Etruscan (but using Roman letters), while the other brother, Vel, prefers to think of himself in Latin terms. Perhaps Arnth was a bit of an Etruscan nationalist, while Vel embraced Roman domination.

It is clear that the disappearance of the Etruscan alphabet differs from that of Babylonian cuneiform in almost all respects. Most importantly, the script itself survived, unlike cuneiform, and was used to write a new language. Linguistically, it was effective as a script for writing Latin, with only very minor modifications. Changes in commerce had little to do with Etruscan's eclipse, and political changes were not of much relevance either, since the Etruscans were never an imperial power. Perhaps the only significant point in common is that both scripts enjoyed cultural prestige – yet this was certainly far greater for Babylonian than for Etruscan.

The death of Rongorongo

Easter Island (Rapanui) is among the most isolated inhabited spots on earth: 3,780 kilometres west of Chile and 2,250 kilometres east-southeast of Pitcairn Island, its nearest inhabited neighbour. In the 1860s, the outside world first became aware – through the visit of French missionaries – that the island had what appeared to be a writing system. 'Rongorongo' means 'chants or recitations' in the Polynesian language of Easter Island, and the word has also been applied to the script, which was, it seems, chanted while being read. However, even as it was being discovered

is poorly known, the content of the Tabula Cortonensis is very incompletely understood. However, names and places and some Etruscan vocabulary words are clear. The tablet is a record of a contract between the Cusu family, to which Petru Scevas belongs, and 15 other people, witnessed by a third group of names, including some of their children and grandchildren. It relates to a sale, or lease, of land including a vineyard, in the plain of Lake Trasimeno, not far from Cortona by outsiders, Rongorongo seems to have been on the edge of extinction, probably due to the catastrophic depopulation of Easter Island caused by labour raids on the island by Peruvian entrepreneurs and the ravages of disease; in the 1860s, some 94 per cent of Easter Islanders either emigrated or died. The missionaries struggled to find any islander who could read Rongorongo.

There are 25 examples of the script on pieces of wood, including driftwood, scattered around the world's museums. These contain somewhere between 14,000 and 17,000 'glyphs', depending on how one chooses to count the more complex signs, engraved with a shark's tooth, a flake of obsidian, or a sharpened bird bone. The signs are mostly stylized outlines of objects or creatures, including a curious 'bird-man' figure. They do not resemble the pictograms of any other script, with the exception, strangely enough, of a few of the signs of the 4,000-year-old Indus Valley script – though this similarity is surely pure coincidence.

Two basic questions about Rongorongo need to be answered. First, is it full writing or some unusual kind of proto-writing, in which the signs acted as a mnemonic to the chanter? By the time that careful research was done on this question, in the 20th century, there were no surviving native chanters, so it was not possible to interrogate a human informant. Based on 19th-century European records of Rongorongo chanting of doubtful reliability, and a purely visual analysis of the signs, many theories have been advanced, and a number of 'decipherments' published, most recently in the 1990s. There is no consensus – as with the undeciphered Indus Valley script – but it seems likely from the research of the leading experts that there is a phonetic system, possibly syllabic, represented in Rongorongo. Certainty about this will most likely forever elude us, because insufficient samples of the script exist (and no more will be discovered, given the effect of the island's warm and moist climate on wood), and because the origin and age of the script are controversial.

12. The Santiago staff, a wooden staff kept at a museum in Santiago in Chile, is the largest and longest example of the Rongorongo script of Easter Island, with 2,300 inscribed characters. This drawing shows the beginning of the inscription. The date of the staff is unknown but is likely to be from the period of the 1770s to 1860s, when the script was certainly in use. Despite several claims to the contrary, Rongorongo has yet to be deciphered

Which leads us to the second question. How was Rongorongo invented? None of the inscriptions is dated. There are therefore three possibilities. First, the islanders independently invented the script, unprompted from outside. Second, they brought the idea from another country such as Peru or China. Lastly, they invented it after the visit of Europeans to Easter Island in 1770, having seen the European writing of the sailors. If Rongorongo did exist before the Europeans came, then Easter Island would be unique among the islands of Polynesia, since there are no known pre-colonial writing systems from Polynesia. If independent invention were to be proved, it would enormously strengthen the position of those who believe in a multiple origin – as opposed to a single origin – of full writing.

There are reasonable arguments for all three positions, but the third possibility – European stimulus – seems somewhat more probable than the other two. If it is correct, though, this would mean that the script was invented some time in the 1770s or after, brought to a fine pitch and more or less abandoned, all within less than 90 years. While certainly conceivable – as witness the disappearance of the Phags-pa script of the Mongolians in less than a century – this scenario is not altogether plausible, though it does accord with the young age of the wood in all surviving Rongorongo inscriptions.

Clearly, the death of Rongorongo – assuming it was full writing – is a unique case in the long history of disappearance of scripts, which cannot really be compared with any other vanished script. Except perhaps in one regard: it reminds us of how protean writing is.

Chapter 4
Decipherment and undeciphered scripts

In ordinary conversation, to decipher someone's 'indecipherable' handwriting means to make sense of the meaning; it does not imply that one can read every single word. In its more technical sense, as applied to ancient scripts, 'deciphered' means different things to different scholars. At one extreme, everyone agrees that the Egyptian hieroglyphs have been deciphered – because every trained Egyptologist would make the same sense of virtually every word of a given hieroglyphic inscription (though their individual translations would still differ, as do all independent translations of the same work from one language into another). At the other extreme, almost everyone agrees that the scripts of the Indus Valley civilization and Easter Island (Rongorongo) are undeciphered – because no scholar can make sense of their inscriptions to the satisfaction of the majority of other specialists. Between these extremes lies a vast spectrum of opinion. In the case of the Mayan glyphs, for example, most scholars agree that a high proportion, as much as 85 per cent, of the inscriptions can be meaningfully read, and yet there remain large numbers of individual glyphs that are contentious or obscure.

In other words, no shibboleth exists by which we judge a script to be 'deciphered' or 'undeciphered'; we should instead speak of *degrees* of decipherment. The most useful criterion is that a proposed decipherment can generate consistent readings from new samples of the script, preferably produced by persons other than the original decipherer, so as to avoid bias. In this sense, the Egyptian hieroglyphs were deciphered in the 1820s by Jean-François Champollion and others; Babylonian cuneiform in the 1850s by Henry Creswicke Rawlinson and others; Linear B in 1952–3 by Michael Ventris and John Chadwick; the Mayan glyphs in the 1950s and after by Yuri Knorosov and others; and the Hittite (Luvian) hieroglyphs of Anatolia during the 20th century by a series of scholars – to name only the most important of the generally accepted decipherments.

This leaves a number of significant undeciphered languages/ scripts, listed in the table on page 54. They fall into three basic categories: an unknown script writing a known language; a known script writing an unknown language; and an unknown script writing an unknown language.

The Mayan glyphs were until the 1950s an example of the first category, since the Mayan languages are still spoken in Central America. The Zapotec script may be, too, if it writes a language related to the modern Zapotec language family of Mexico. Even Rongorongo may belong to this first category, since it almost certainly writes a Polynesian language related to the Tahitian-influenced Polynesian language spoken today on Easter Island. Etruscan writing exemplifies the second category, since the Etruscan script is basically the same as the Greek alphabet, while the Etruscan language is not related to any known language. The Indus script belongs to the third category, since the signs on the seals and other inscriptions bear no resemblance to any other script, and the language of the Indus Valley civilization does not appear to have survived – unless, as many scholars have speculated, it is an ancestor of the Dravidian languages such as

Name of script	Where found	Earliest known	Script known?	Language lnown?
Proto-Elamite	Iran/Iraq	c. 3000 BC	Partially	No
Indus	Pakistan/N.W. India	c. 2500 BC	No	*
'Pseudo-hieroglyphic'	Byblos (Lebanon)	2nd mill. BC	No	No
Linear A	Crete	18th cent. BC	Partially	No
Phaistos Disc	Phaistos (Crete)	18th cent. BC	No	No
Etruscan	N. Italy	8th cent. BC	Yes	No
Olmec	Meso-America	c. 900 BC	Partially	No
Zapotec	Meso-America	c. 600 BC	Partially	Partially
Meroitic	Meroe (Sudan)	c. 200 BC	Yes	No
Isthmian	Meso-America	c. AD 150	*	*
Rongorongo	Easter Island	pre-19th cent. AD	No	Partially

13. **In this table of the major undeciphered scripts, an asterisk ***
indicates cases in which there is no scholarly consensus on the
nature of the script and/or its underlying language

Tamil and Brahui, spoken predominantly in south India but also in
parts of Pakistan.

Approaches to decipherment

Ventris, perhaps the greatest of the decipherers, summarized the
decipherment process masterfully, as follows:

> Each operation needs to be planned in three phases: an exhaustive
> *analysis* of the signs, words and contexts in all the available
> inscriptions, designed to extract every possible clue as to the spelling
> system, meaning and language structure; an experimental
> *substitution* of phonetic values to give possible words and inflections
> in a known or postulated language; and a decisive *check*, preferably

with the aid of virgin material, to ensure that the apparent results are not due to fantasy, coincidence or circular reasoning.

Although successful decipherments do not simply follow this sequence, they always involve three processes: analysis, substitution, and check.

What are the minimum conditions for a high degree of decipherment to be feasible? According to Ventris again, 'Prerequisites are that the material should be large enough for the analysis to yield usable results, and (in the case of an unreadable script without bilinguals or identifiable proper names) that the concealed language should be related to one which we already know.' Lack of material means that without further discoveries there is at present no prospect of deciphering the Olmec and Isthmian scripts from Mexico, the Phaistos Disc from Crete, and the Byblos 'pseudo-hieroglyphic' script from Lebanon, among those mentioned in the table of undeciphered scripts. Linear B was decipherable – despite lacking a 'Rosetta Stone' bilingual with identifiable proper names – because the concealed language was discovered (by Ventris) to be archaic Greek.

Two elements of an unknown script usually yield up their secrets without too much effort. The first is the direction of the writing: from left to right or from right to left, from top to bottom or from bottom to top. Clues to the direction include the position of unfilled space in the text, the way in which characters sometimes crowd (on the left or on the right), and the direction in which pictographic signs face (as in Egyptian hieroglyphic). However, there are certain scripts that are written 'boustrophedon', a term from the Greek for 'as the ox turns', when ploughing: in other words first from left to right (say), then from right to left, then again from left to right, and so on. There are even reverse-boustrophedon scripts, in which the writer turned the original document through 180 degrees come the end of each line; Rongorongo is an example of this.

14. **Michael Ventris (1922–56) announced the decipherment of Linear B in 1952. Trained as an architect, he was also a phenomenal linguist who became fascinated by Linear B as a schoolboy. The photograph shows him at his Linear B drawing board in mid-1953, just after his decipherment was confirmed by the discovery of a new tablet in Greece**

The second element is the system of counting. Numerals frequently stand out graphically from the rest of the text, especially if they are used for calculations (which helpfully suggests that the non-numerical signs next to the numerals are likely to stand for counted objects or people). Easily visible numerals are a particular feature of the Linear B and Mayan scripts and, among the undeciphered scripts, of the proto-Elamite script. A numerical system is obvious in the Etruscan script, Linear A, and the Zapotec and Isthmian scripts, and fairly clear in the Indus script; but it seems to be largely absent from the Meroitic script and Rongorongo, and not at all evident in the Phaistos Disc. Of course, in working out a system of ancient numerals, decipherers have to be aware that it may differ radically from our decimal system. The Babylonians, for instance, used a sexagesimal system, from which we inherit 60 seconds in a minute and 360 degrees in a circle, and no zero; the Maya had a vigesimal system, increasing in multiples of 20, and a shell symbol for zero.

More challenging than the direction of writing or numerals is the analysis of the sign system as a whole. Suppose you were unfamiliar with the Roman alphabet. If you were to take a typical chapter of an ordinary novel printed in English, it would be a fairly straightforward matter, by careful study and comparison of the thousands of characters in the text, to work out that they could be classified into a set of signs: 26 lower-case ones and the same number of upper-case signs, though you might wonder whether letters with ascenders like b, d, f, h, k should be classified with the lower-case or with the upper-case letters—plus sundry other signs: punctuation marks, numerals, and logograms like @ and £. Now imagine that the same text is handwritten. Immediately, the task of isolating the signs is far harder, because the letters are joined up and different writers write the same letter in different ways, also differently from its printed equivalent, and not always distinctly.

The same sign written in a variant form is known in epigraphy as an *allograph*. A key challenge for the epigrapher/decipherer – who naturally cannot be sure in advance that different-looking signs are in fact allographs of only one sign – is how to distinguish signs that are genuinely different, such as 'l' and 'I', from signs that are probably allographs, such as printed 'a' and handwritten '*a*' (not to mention 'A'). Judging by deciphered scripts, an undeciphered script may easily contain three or four allographs of the same basic sign. The would-be decipherer needs to be able to work out, say, which of the stick figures in this enigmatic cipher-text from the Sherlock Holmes story 'The Adventure of the Dancing Men', are allographs:

Unless epigraphers can distinguish allographs with a fair degree of confidence, generally by comparing their contexts in many very similar inscriptions, they cannot classify the phonetic signs in a script (its signary) correctly, neither can they establish the total number of signs in the signary. Classification is self-evidently crucial to decipherment, but the number of signs is almost as important. Alphabets like English and consonantal scripts like Arabic mostly number between 20 and about 40 signs; Hebrew has 22 signs, English 26, Arabic 28, and Cyrillic 43 signs, 33 of which are used in modern Russian. (Some consonant-rich languages of the northern Caucasus have more than 40 alphabetic signs.) Essentially syllabic scripts, in which the signs stand for syllables not vowels and consonants, number between 40 and about 85–90 basic signs; Persian has 40 signs, Japanese around 50 syllabic *kana*, and Linear B 60 basic signs. More complex scripts, which mix a relatively small set of phonetic signs with large numbers of logograms, such as Egyptian and Mayan hieroglyphic, and Babylonian cuneiform, number many hundreds of signs, or even several thousands of signs, as in Chinese characters and the Japanese *kanji* borrowed from Chinese.

Once we know the size of an undeciphered script's signary, we can therefore get a fair idea of whether it is an alphabetic/consonantal script, a syllabary, or a mixture of syllables and logograms, i.e. a logosyllabic script – without having any idea of the phonetic values of the signs. This broad system of classifying scripts was first recognized in the 1870s and was taken up by decipherers in the 20th century. For instance, the decipherers of Ugaritic cuneiform quickly realized that with a signary of only 30, Ugaritic could not be a logosyllabic script like Babylonian cuneiform. Ventris, from the size of the Linear B signary, convinced himself that Linear B was a syllabic script, not an alphabet or a logosyllabic script, which was an important step in the direction of decipherment. A similar line of argument has been useful in narrowing the range of possibilities for the still-undeciphered scripts: there appear to be about 60 phonetic signs in Linear A, and perhaps 55 in

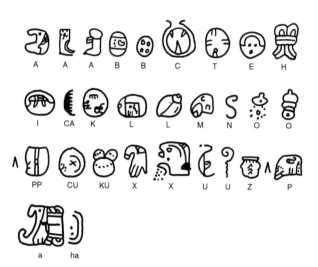

15. This so-called Mayan 'alphabet' is from the surviving copy of an original manuscript written in the 16th century by a Spanish priest, Diego de Landa, who worked among the Maya in the Yucatan. In the 1950s and after, it provided the key to the decipherment of the phonetic Mayan glyphs. In the 1560s, Landa, later bishop of Yucatan, interrogated a senior Maya man about his script. However, Landa spoke in Spanish, while pointing to the different symbols of the script, and misunderstood some of what he was told by his informant. Assuming that the Maya wrote in an alphabet, like Spanish, Landa did not grasp that the Mayan phonetic signs were essentially syllabic with an admixture of pure vowels, although he obviously understood that certain signs, such as 'CA' and 'KU', represented syllables. And of course he did not even begin to grasp that most Mayan glyphs (many hundreds) were not phonetic signs but rather logograms, and that the Mayan script as a whole is a logosyllabic script with little resemblance to an alphabet. Ironically, given his inadvertent contribution to the decipherment, Landa proceeded to burn any Mayan manuscripts he could lay hands on, as being works of the devil

16. This Classic Mayan ceramic vessel, dating from the 5th century AD, was excavated in Rio Azul, Guatemala. The glyph in the centre (on the left) stands for 'cacao', which was a key ingredient of a favourite Mayan maize and chocolate drink. The Mayan word is spelt phonetically as *ka-ka-w(a)* with three phonetic syllabic signs, one of them partly repeated – within one glyph. Chemical tests have detected cacao residues at the bottom of the pot

Rongorongo, which, if true, would imply that both scripts are syllabaries.

If the signs of an undeciphered script can be correctly classified, with the allographs accurately identified – a challenging condition, it has to be said – each sign can be given a number and each inscription written in terms of a sequence of numbers instead of the usual graphic symbols. The inscription can also be classified by computer in a *concordance*, that is a catalogue organized by sign (not by inscription) that under each sign lists every inscription containing the particular sign. (Literary concordances are used by scholars to research every instance of a particular word in, say, the entire works of Shakespeare.) Concordances offer important possibilities for analysing the distribution of signs. Once all of the text data has been computerized in a concordance, one can ask the computer to calculate the relative sign frequencies (for instance, which is the commonest sign, and which is the least common?), or to list all the inscriptions in which a particular combination of signs occurs. If one suspects this combination of representing, say, a certain word or proper name, one can then analyse in exactly which contexts (at the beginning of inscriptions, in the middle words, next to which other signs?) the combination occurs – within every inscription in a corpus.

Although such frequency analysis has been done by computer in the case of the Linear A, Meroitic, and Indus script corpuses, the truth is that computers have made little impact on archaeological decipherment. Electronic computers came along more or less too late for Ventris (who anyway does not appear to have been interested in computing), yet none of the decipherers of recent decades has found computers as useful as they hoped. One reason is the difficulty of discriminating between signs and their allographs, which is still a matter of human judgement; another is the great graphical complexity of, say, the Mayan script, which does not lend itself to the black-and-white, discrete nature of numerical classification; yet another reason, more general, is that there is not really enough text available in the undeciphered scripts for computerized statistical techniques to prove decisive. On the whole, successful decipherment has turned out to require a synthesis of logic and intuition based on wide linguistic, archaeological, and cultural knowledge that computers do not (and presumably cannot) possess.

Deciphering Egyptian hieroglyphic

The Rosetta Stone is a slab of compact granitic stone weighing some three-quarters of a ton and measuring just 114 centimetres in height, 72 centimetres in width and 28 centimetres in thickness. From the moment of its discovery in 1799 by French soldiers of Napoleon Bonaparte stationed at Rosetta (modern Rashid), on the Nile Delta coast of Egypt, it was clear that the inscription on the stone was written in three different scripts, the bottom one being Greek and the top one (which was badly damaged) Egyptian hieroglyphic. Sandwiched in between was a script about which little was known. It clearly did not resemble the Greek alphabet, but it seemed to bear some slight resemblance to the hieroglyphic. However, unlike the hieroglyphic, the unknown script had no cartouches: groups of signs encircled with an oval ring, which reminded the soldiers of the cartridges (*cartouches*) in their guns. Today, of course, we know the middle script to be demotic, a cursive form of hieroglyphic.

The first step towards a decipherment was obviously to translate the Greek inscription. It turned out to be a decree passed by a general council of priests from all parts of Egypt that assembled at Memphis on the first anniversary of the coronation of Ptolemy V Epiphanes, king of all Egypt, on 27 March 196 BC. The names Ptolemy, Alexander, Alexandria, among others, occurred in the Greek inscription. The very last sentence read:

17. The Rosetta Stone, discovered in Egypt in 1799, records a royal decree of 196 BC in three scripts (reading from the top): Egyptian hieroglyphic, Egyptian demotic, and Greek alphabetic

> This decree shall be inscribed on a stela of hard stone in sacred
> [hieroglyphic] and native [demotic] and Greek characters and set
> up in each of the first, second and third [-rank] temples beside the
> image of the ever-living king.

Then scholars turned their attention to the demotic script. (The hieroglyphic section was too damaged to appear promising.) They knew from this final statement that the three inscriptions, written in Greek and Egyptian, were equivalent in meaning, a bilingual, even if not 'word for word' translations. So they searched for a name such as Ptolemy, by isolating repeated groups of demotic symbols located in roughly the same position as the known occurrences of Ptolemy in the Greek inscription. Having found these groups, they noticed that the names in demotic seemed to be written alphabetically, as in the Greek inscription. They were able to draw up a tentative demotic alphabet. Certain other demotic words, such as 'Greek', 'Egypt', 'temple', could now be identified using this demotic alphabet. It looked as though the entire demotic script might be alphabetic.

Unfortunately it was not. The first scholars could proceed no further, because they could not rid themselves of the idea that the demotic inscription was an alphabet – in stark contrast to the hieroglyphic inscription. This they took to be non-phonetic, an essentially pictographic script symbolizing only ideas, often mystical, as described by commentators in classical antiquity such as Horapollo (writing in the 4th century AD or later) and Renaissance scholars such as the Jesuit Athanasius Kircher. The difference in appearance between the hieroglyphic and demotic signs, and the weight of traditional thinking about Egyptian hieroglyphs, convinced the scholars of 1800 that the invisible principles of the two scripts, hieroglyphic and demotic, must be wholly different: one non-phonetic, the other alphabetic.

Thomas Young

The person who broke this mould was the Englishman Thomas Young. A remarkable polymath – linguist, physician, and physicist, whose wave theory of light was a key contribution to 19th-century physics – Young started work on the Rosetta Stone in 1814. He began with what Ventris later called the 'exhaustive analysis' phase of decipherment. After painstaking comparison of the demotic and hieroglyphic sections in the Rosetta Stone – and of the hieratic and hieroglyphic sections of papyrus manuscripts – Young noted what he called 'a striking resemblance' between some demotic signs and 'the corresponding hieroglyphs'. He remarked that 'none of these characters [the hieroglyphs] could be reconciled, without inconceivable violence, to the forms of any imaginable alphabet'. He therefore concluded that the demotic script was a *mixture* of alphabetic signs and other, hieroglyphic-type signs.

Then Young went further, acting on a suggestion made by earlier scholars that the cartouches contained royal or religious names. There were six cartouches in the Rosetta Stone's hieroglyphic inscription, which clearly had to contain the name Ptolemy. Young assumed that Ptolemy, though written in hieroglyphic, was spelt alphabetically. His reason was that Ptolemy was a foreign (Greek) name, non-Egyptian, and therefore it would not be spelt like an Egyptian name, non-phonetically. By way of analogy, in the Chinese script foreign names were known to be written phonetically in Chinese characters with a special sign to indicate this fact. (English-speakers indicate some foreign words in writing with their own 'special sign' – italicization.) Might not the cartouche be the ancient Egyptian hieroglyphic equivalent of the special sign accompanying groups of Chinese characters?

If so, the phonetic hieroglyphs in the Ptolemy cartouche could be matched up with the alphabetic letters p, t, o, l, m e, s, spelling Ptolemy in the Greek inscription of the Rosetta Stone. Using this idea, Young moved on to what Ventris called the 'experimental substitution of phonetic values' phase of decipherment. Young was able to assign phonetic values (*p*, *t*, *m*, etc.) to a number of hieroglyphs. Many, though not all, were correct. Over the next three years, 1815–18, he made solid contributions to the decipherment of hieroglyphic and demotic. For example, he identified hieroglyphic plural markers, various numerical notations, and a special sign (semicircle with oval) for marking feminine names like Berenice, queen of Ptolemy III.

Eventually, however, Young stalled. The spell of classical and Renaissance tradition was a strong one. While he could accept that hieroglyphic employed an alphabet to spell foreign names, he was convinced that the remaining hieroglyphs, the major part used to write the Egyptian language (rather than names and words borrowed from Greek), were *non*-phonetic. Young's burgeoning 'hieroglyphic alphabet' would therefore not apply, he assumed, to the bulk of the hieroglyphic script. He had correctly understood parts of the hieroglyphic and demotic writing systems, but he would not be the person to break the hieroglyphic code. In Ventris's terms, Young was unable to move convincingly to the third phase of decipherment, the 'decisive check' of his tentative results using virgin material, because his analysis was incomplete and in parts faulty.

Jean-François Champollion

The full decipherment was the work of the Frenchman Jean-François Champollion, who announced it in 1823. Born during the French Revolution, he was unable to attend early school. Instead, he received private tuition in Greek and Latin, and by the age of nine, it is said, he could read Homer and Virgil. Moving to Grenoble to attend the Lycée, he came into contact with the mathematician and physicist Jean-Baptiste Fourier, who had been secretary of Napoleon's Egyptian expedition. It was Fourier who launched the twelve-year-old Champollion into Egyptology. In 1807, aged not yet 17, Champollion presented a paper on the Coptic

18. Jean-François Champollion (1790–1832) announced the decipherment of Egyptian hieroglyphic in 1823. This portrait painting of c. 1823, attributed to Mme de Rumilly, shows him holding his initial 'Tableau des Signes Phonétiques', published in 1822, which gave hieroglyphic and demotic equivalents for the letters of the Greek alphabet

etymology of Egyptian place-names in the works of Greek and Latin authors. Coptic was the final stage of the language of ancient Egypt, used by the Egyptian church from around the time of Christ. Three years later, after studying oriental languages in Paris in addition to Coptic, Champollion returned to Grenoble and immersed himself in serious study of Egyptian civilization.

In 1819, Young published his ideas on the Egyptian scripts in a pioneering *Supplement to the Encyclopaedia Britannica* (4th edition). He had earlier communicated them by letter to Champollion. But Champollion at first ignored them and continued to believe that the hieroglyphs were entirely *non*-phonetic; in 1821 he published a brief text to this effect. Then he changed his mind, probably as a result of reading Young's *Supplement*. He and Young were undoubtedly rivals, and there is still doubt as to how much Champollion was influenced by Young's work; he certainly took pains to diminish it in his chief book on Egyptian writing. However, there can be no question about Champollion's originality and rigour, which was based on a knowledge of Egypt and its languages, including Coptic, far superior to Young's.

The key to further progress was a copy of a bilingual Egyptian obelisk inscription sent to Paris by the antiquarian William Bankes around January 1822. It came from Britain, where the obelisk had been dispatched after its removal by Bankes from the island of Philae near Aswan. The base block inscription was in Greek, the column inscription in hieroglyphic. In the Greek the names of Ptolemy and Cleopatra were mentioned; in the hieroglyphs only two cartouches occurred – presumably representing the names written on the base. One of the cartouches was almost identical to one form of the cartouche of Ptolemy on the Rosetta Stone:

Rosetta Stone   Philae obelisk

There was also a shorter version of the Ptolemy cartouche on the Rosetta Stone:

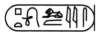

Champollion decided that the shorter version spelt Ptolemy, while the longer (Rosetta) cartouche must involve some royal title, tacked onto Ptolemy's name. Following Young, he now assumed that Ptolemy was spelt alphabetically. He proceeded to guess the phonetic values of the hieroglyphs of the second cartouche on the Philae obelisk:

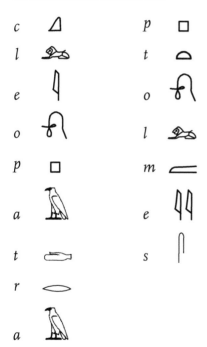

There were four signs in common, those with the values *l*, *e*, *o*, *p*, but the phonetic value *t* was represented differently. Champollion deduced correctly that the two signs for *t* were homophones, that is different signs with the same phonetic value (compare in English **J**ill and **G**ill, defen**c**e and defen**s**e).

The real test, however, was whether the new phonetic values when applied to other inscriptions, would produce sensible names (the 'check' phase of decipherment mentioned by Ventris).
Champollion tried the following cartouche:

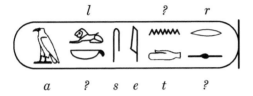

Substituting phonetic values produced *Al?se?tr?*. Champollion guessed Alksentrs = Greek Alexandros (Alexander) – again the two signs for *k/c* (⟨⟩ and ⟨⟩) are homophonous, as are the signs for *s* (●— and |).

He went on to identify the cartouches of other rulers of non-Egyptian origin, such as *Kesrs* (Caesar) and *Brneka* (Berenice).
Her cartouche – already identified by Young, with its two-sign feminine termination – looks like this:

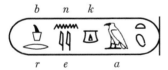

These early efforts of Champollion, announced in October 1822, were based on the premise that *non-Egyptian* names and words in both demotic and hieroglyphic were spelt alphabetically. This was how he worked out a table of phonetic signs, in the manner of Young's 'hieroglyphic alphabet', but much fuller and more accurate than his rival's. Champollion did not initially expect his phonetic values to apply to the names of Egyptian-origin rulers (pre-Alexander), which he persisted in thinking would be spelt non-phonetically. Even less did he expect his 'decipherment' to apply to the entire hieroglyphic system. The hoary idea, dating from classical antiquity, that Egyptian hieroglyphs for the most part expressed only ideas, rather than sounds *and* ideas, still possessed Champollion's mind, as it had Young's. Not until April 1823 did Champollion announce that he understood the principles of hieroglyphic as a writing system.

The shift in Champollion's conception of hieroglyphic in 1822–3 started when he received copies of various reliefs and inscriptions from ancient Egyptian temples in September 1822. One of them, from the temple of Abu Simbel in Nubia, contained intriguing cartouches. They appeared to write the same name in a variety of ways, the simplest being:

Champollion wondered if his new alphabet, derived from much later Graeco-Roman inscriptions, might apply to this set of purely Egyptian inscriptions. The last two signs were familiar to him, having the phonetic value *s*. Using his knowledge of Coptic, he guessed that the first sign had the value *re*, which was the Coptic word for 'sun' – the object apparently symbolized by the sign. Did an ancient Egyptian ruler with a name that resembled *R(e)?ss* exist? Champollion, steeped in his passion for ancient Egypt, immediately thought of Ramesses, a king of the 19th dynasty mentioned in a well-known Greek history of Egypt written by a Ptolemaic historian, Manetho. If he was correct, then the sign 𓏶 must have the phonetic value *m*. (He assumed that hieroglyphic did not represent vowels, except in foreign names.)

Encouragement came from a second inscription:

Two of these signs were 'known'; the first, an ibis, was a symbol of the god Thoth (inventor of writing). Then the name had to be Thothmes, a king of the 18th dynasty also mentioned by Manetho. The Rosetta Stone appeared to confirm the value of 𓏠. The sign occurred there, again with 𓏏, as part of a group of hieroglyphs with the Greek translation 'genethlia', meaning 'birthday'. Champollion was at once reminded of the Coptic for 'give birth', 'mise'.

Champollion was only half right about the spelling of Ramesses: 𓏠 does not have the phonetic value *m*, as he thought, it has the *bi*consonantal value *ms* (as implied by the Coptic 'mise'). Champollion was as yet unaware of this complexity. For some months after his success in deciphering Ramesses and other Egyptian-origin names, he resisted the idea that the hieroglyphic system as a whole had phonetic elements. He never said what finally changed his mind in late 1822, but it was probably a combination of factors. For one thing, he learnt with surprise from a French scholar of Chinese that there were phonetic elements not only in foreign names written in Chinese characters but also in indigenous words. For another, it struck him that there were only 66 signs among the 1419 hieroglyphic symbols on the Rosetta Stone; if the hieroglyphs truly were symbols of words and ideas, then many more than 66 signs would have been expected, each a logogram representing a different word. The small ratio of signs to symbols implied instead a small set of phonetic signs mixed with the logograms.

Once he had accepted that the hieroglyphs were a mixture of phonetic signs and logograms, Champollion could decipher the second half of the long cartouche of Ptolemy on the Philae obelisk. That is:

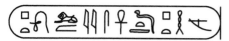

According to the Greek inscription, the entire cartouche meant 'Ptolemy living for ever, beloved of Ptah' (Ptah was the creator god of Memphis). In Coptic, the word for 'life' or 'living' was 'onkh'; this was thought to be derived from an ancient Egyptian word 'ankh' represented by the sign ♀ (a logogram). Presumably the next signs 🗂 meant 'ever' and contained a *t* sound, given that the sign △ was now known to have the phonetic value *t*. With help from Greek and Coptic, the ↰ could be assigned the phonetic value *dj*, giving a rough ancient Egyptian pronunciation *djet*, meaning 'for ever'. (The other sign was silent, a kind of classificatory logogram called a determinative; it symbolized 'flat land'.)

Of the remaining signs 🗂 ⚬ ↳, the first was now known to stand for *p* and the second for *t* – the first two sounds of Ptah; and so the third sign could be given the approximate phonetic value *h*. The fourth sign – another logogram – was therefore assumed to mean 'beloved'. Coptic once more came in useful to assign a pronunciation: the Coptic word for 'love' was known to be 'mere', and so the pronunciation of the fourth sign was thought to be *mer*. So, in sum, Champollion arrived at the following rough approximation of the famous cartouche (guessing at the unwritten vowels): *Ptolmes ankh djet Ptah mer* – 'Ptolemy living for ever, beloved of Ptah'.

Chapter 5
How writing systems work

Europeans and Americans of ordinary literacy must recognize and write around 52 alphabetic signs (26 capital letters and their lower-case equivalents), as well as numerals, punctuation marks, and a small number of logograms. Literate Japanese readers, by contrast, with the most complicated writing system in the world, are supposed to know and be able to write two different syllabaries ('kana') with about 50 signs each, plus just under 2,000 further signs ('kanji') taken from Chinese characters, which are generally logograms. Those who are highly educated must recognize many more kanji than this. Before the Second World War, there were some 7,500 kanji in the type-font of Japanese newspapers; even today, newspapers use about 3,200–3,300 kanji.

These two situations for readers and writers in Europe/America and in Japan, appear to be poles apart. In fact, the different writing systems resemble each other more than appears. Contrary to what many people think, all scripts that are full writing operate on one basic principle. Both alphabets and the Chinese and Japanese scripts use symbols to represent sounds; and all writing systems mix such phonetic symbols with logograms. What differs between writing systems – apart from the forms of their signs, of course – are the proportions of the phonetic signs and the logograms.

Classification of writing systems

The higher the proportion of phonetic representation in a script, the easier it is to guess the pronunciation of a word from its spelling. The schematic diagram below, devised by the specialist in Japanese J. Marshall Unger, indicates the proportions of phoneticism and logography in a range of scripts. On the extreme left, the International Phonetic Alphabet aims to be purely phonetic. Invented in the late 19th century, its symbols, based on the Roman and Greek alphabets with the addition of some special symbols and diacritical marks, are intended to be able to write any language with a strict one-to-one correspondence between symbol and sound. On the extreme right, cryptographic codes are purely logographic.

Among the writing systems used to write spoken languages, the Finnish script on the left has the highest proportion of phoneticism, while the Japanese on the right has the lowest proportion. Hebrew and Arabic, which in their original forms did not mark vowels (though their modern forms do), lie in the middle. Japanese is adjudged to be slightly more logographic than Chinese, because many Japanese kanji can take multiple variant readings as a result of their complex history of being borrowed from Chinese to

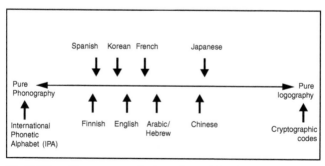

19. All full writing systems mix phonetic symbols with logograms, but the proportions vary. See the text for a fuller explanation

write a different language. On the other hand, as Unger notes, Japanese uses the highly phonetic kana syllabary, which has no direct equivalent in Chinese (which nevertheless has syllabic signs). So some scholars might wish to reverse Japanese and Chinese in the diagram.

The position of Korean is especially interesting. In Korea, a primarily phonetic script was for centuries in competition with a primarily logographic script. The Korean writing system was once founded on the Chinese characters ('hanja') but is now Hangul, the basically alphabetic system introduced in the 15th century, originally consisting of 28 signs that today consists of 40 signs. Yet hanja have not entirely disappeared. In North Korea, the Communist ruler Kim Il Sung banned hanja until 1964, when they were reintroduced for reasons that are not clear; 2,000 hanja began to be taught to pre-collegiate students. In South Korea, the government planned a ban on hanja in 1948, relented in 1949 provided that hanja were accompanied by Hangul, then in 1950 settled for a mixture of hanja and Hangul. In 1955, hanja were abolished, but in 1964 they came back, 1,300 hanja being introduced into elementary and secondary-school textbooks. Again, in 1968, Hangul was decreed to be the only South Korean script, and school texts were written exclusively in Hangul in 1970. However, in 1972, some 1,800 hanja were reintroduced into schools. Although they are still taught to schoolchildren, there is little opportunity to read hanja, which today appear only in newspapers for writing some personal names and to a small extent in university textbooks. Korean hanja-based writing (not shown in the diagram) would lie slightly to the left of Chinese.

From the above discussion, it should be plain that there is no such thing as a 'pure' writing system, that is, a full writing system capable of expressing meaning entirely through alphabetic letters or entirely through syllabic signs or entirely through logograms. All systems are mixtures of phonetic and logographic representation. How best to classify writing systems is therefore a controversial matter.

Thus some scholars, notably Ignace J. Gelb in his influential *A Study of Writing*, deny the existence of alphabets prior to the Greek alphabet, because the Phoenician script marked only consonants, no vowels. This is also true of the Hebrew and Arabic scripts, before they acquired a system of three basic signs for marking vowels. These diacritical dots and small strokes, known as vowel 'points', added above and below the consonant preceding the vowel, were developed in AD 600–1000 to indicate the correct pronunciation of religious texts. For example, فَوْتُ ٱلْغَنِيِّ فَإِنْ لِغَرِمِثْلَ حَيَاتِهِ رَعِيثُهُ فِى ٱلذُّلِّ عَيْنَ عَاتِهِ. Gelb lumps Phoenician, Aramaic, Hebrew, and Arabic together as West Semitic syllabaries, not alphabets, on the grounds that their signs stand for consonants with inherent vowels. 'If the alphabet is defined as a system of signs expressing single sounds of speech, then the first alphabet which can justifiably be so called is the Greek alphabet', Gelb maintains. However, the majority of scholars are content with common usage (as is this book), and regard the Phoenician, Aramaic, Hebrew, and Arabic scripts as alphabets.

Indian scripts, such as Devanagari (used for Sanskrit and Hindi) and Grantha (used for Tamil), are more resistant to classification. Non-Indians sometimes call them alphabets, yet Indians generally refer to the *akshara*, a Sanskrit word defining a modified consonantal syllabary, in which most (though not all) vowels are represented by diacritics attached to the consonants. Are Indian scripts alphabets or syllabaries? Descended from the early Brahmi script, which was probably influenced by the Aramaic script, they are in some ways alphabetic, in others closer to syllabic. Well over 2,000 years ago, the ancient Indians used their sophisticated knowledge of phonology and grammar to organize their signs differently from Aramaic. The Brahmi signs are classified in accordance with place of articulation in the mouth: vowels and diphthongs come first, then consonants in the following logical order: gutturals, palatals, retroflexes, dentals, labials, semi-vowels, and spirants. Yet often it is a syllable that the sign represents; consonant signs that express inherent vowels, in other words syllables, are extremely important in Indian writing systems: for example, the sign for 'b' in Bengali represents the sound *bo* (with a short o) and is conventionally written as 'ba'.

Perhaps Indian scripts might be classified as consonantal syllabaries. Yet, such a label would be confusing, because the scripts also mark certain vowels separately from consonants, as in alphabets. 'What then are Indian scripts?' asks one specialist, Albertine Gaur, in *A History of Writing*. 'They have been variously described as alphabetical, consonantal, or an imperfect attempt to convert a consonantal script into an alphabet.' In Gaur's opinion, 'None of these descriptions can really be justified. Indian scripts are from their recorded beginnings clearly syllabic.'

Despite such difficulties, classifying labels are useful to remind us of the predominant nature of different writing systems. The tree diagram on page 79 divides a representative selection of writing systems according to their nature, not according to their age; it does *not* show how one system may have given rise to another historically. (The dashed lines indicate historical or possible influence of one system upon another.)

Linear B is labelled predominantly syllabic, with most of its signs representing the combination consonant-plus-vowel. Mayan glyphs are logosyllabic, because they have a high proportion of logograms, mixed with a smaller set of syllabic signs. Egyptian hieroglyphic is logoconsonantal, because its high proportion of logograms is mixed with a set of 24 consonantal signs but no vowel signs. The Arabic script is a consonantal alphabet, in which a set of 28 consonantal signs predominates over vowel marking (with 'points'). Finnish is a phonemic alphabet, in which the signs predominantly represent phonemes, the smallest contrastive units in the sound system of a language. (Examples of vowel phonemes in English are /e/ and /a/ in the words 'set' and 'sat', while English consonantal phonemes include /b/ and /p/ in the words 'bat' and 'pat'.) English, however, is considered a logophonemic alphabet,

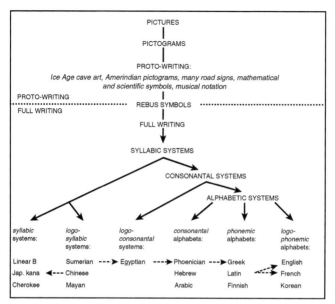

20. Writing systems can be classified into their predominant linguistic type, e.g. 'syllabic' or 'logoconsonantal'. However, the particular labels shown in this diagram are not universally agreed. See the text for a fuller explanation

because its spelling is far removed from phonemic representation: the same English letter represents several different sounds and vice versa. English spelling is strongly influenced by the historical evolution of English words. Indian scripts are omitted here, since their classification is contentious.

Linear B: a syllabic script

To understand how syllabic writing works, we shall look at two celebrated Linear B tablets. The first is from Knossos in Crete, and was discovered by Arthur Evans. It shows pictograms of horse-heads, accompanied by syllabic signs and numerals (the

21. This Linear B tablet from ancient Knossos in Crete counts horses. See the text for an explanation

simple vertical strokes), which count the horses. Of the four horse-heads in the middle and on the right of the tablet, two have manes and two do not. The ones without manes, foals presumably, are preceded by the same word, written as a pair of signs:

$$ \daleth \ + $$

Presumably, the word was added by the Minoan scribe more than three millennia ago to make absolutely clear that the maneless pictogram was a *foal* and not an adult animal.

According to the Linear B syllabary, the two signs read *po-lo*, meaning 'foal'. The tablet can then be read as:

horses 2	*polo* foals
polo foals 2	horses 4

During the decipherment of Linear B, this tablet provided an important clue to the language behind the script, which turned out to be Greek. The classical Greek word for young horse or foal is 'pōlos', and its dual form, meaning two foals, is 'pōlo'. In fact the English word 'foal' is from the same source as Greek 'pōlos'.

The second tablet, drawn here by Michael Ventris, is from mainland Greece, discovered in the archives of the ancient palace

A𐀵𐀀𐀐𐀩𐀯𐀍𐀸𐀐 𐀴 𐀡 2

tiripode aikeu keresijo weke   2

(tripod cauldron of Cretan
workmanship of the *aikeu* type 2)

A𐀴𐀪, 𐀁𐀕, 𐀡𐀆, 𐀃𐀺𐀸 1

tiripo eme pode owowe   1

(tripod cauldron with a single handle
on one foot 1)

A𐀴𐀪, 𐀐𐀩𐀯𐀍, 𐀸𐀐

tiripo keresijo weke

(tripod cauldron of Cretan workmanship)

𐀀𐀢 𐀐𐀏𐀄𐀕𐀜 𐀐𐀩𐀀

apu kekaumeno kerea

(burnt at the legs)

𐀐𐀵 𐀥 3

qeto   3

(wine jars 3)

𐀇𐀞, 𐀕𐀽𐀁, 𐀤𐀵𐀫𐀸 1

dipa mezoe qetorowe   1

(larger-sized goblet with four handles 1)

𐀇𐀞𐀁 𐀕𐀽𐀁 𐀴𐀪𐀺𐀁 2

dipae mezoe tiriowe   2

(larger-sized goblet with three handles 2)

𐀇𐀞, 𐀕𐀹𐀍 𐀤𐀵𐀫𐀸 1

dipa mewijo qetorowe   1

(smaller-sized goblet with four handles 1)

𐀇𐀞, 𐀕𐀹𐀍, 𐀴𐀪𐀍𐀸 1

dipa mewijo tirijowe   1

(smaller-sized goblet with three handles 1)

𐀇𐀞, 𐀕𐀹𐀍, 𐀀𐀜𐀸 1

dipa mewijo anowe   1

(smaller-sized goblet without a handle 1)

22. This Linear B tablet from ancient Pylos in Greece counts vessels. Its discovery confirmed the decipherment of Linear B in 1953. See the text for an explanation

at Pylos believed to have been that of King Nestor, one of the characters in Homer's account of the Trojan War. It counts not horses, but vessels of various kinds and conditions: tripod cauldrons, wine jars, and goblets. The pictograms of these objects are accompanied by descriptive words and phrases in Linear B. Most of these are spelt with consonant-vowel signs, for example the three signs for *ti-ri-po* meaning 'tripod cauldron', the two signs for *qe-to* meaning 'wine jar', and the two signs for *di-pa* meaning 'goblet'; but a few words also use pure vowel signs, for example the pure vowel *a* at the beginning of *a-no-we*, meaning 'without a handle'.

This tablet, revealed by its discoverer Carl Blegen in 1953, after Ventris had announced his decipherment of Linear B in 1952, caused excitement and proved decisive in confirming the correctness of the decipherment. It even suggested a link to Homer, since the word 'dipa' had to be the archaic Greek word for the vessel called 'depas' in Homeric Greek. Was it too far-fetched to associate the four-handled goblet noted in Nestor's palace archives with the cup described by Homer in the *Iliad*, before Nestor sets off for the war? It was 'a magnificent cup adorned with golden studs ... It had four handles ... Anyone else would have found it difficult to shift the cup from the table when full, but Nestor, old as he was, could lift it without trouble.' At any rate, when Ventris published his drawing of the tablet and its signs in 1954, he provocatively entitled his article, 'King Nestor's four-handled cups'. (To his former classics master at school, he wrote jokingly: 'Not quite the Greek you taught me, I'm afraid!')

Egyptian hieroglyphic: a logoconsonantal script

Ancient Egyptian writing is not syllabic; it uses a fairly small set of consonantal signs combined with hundreds of logograms. Many of the hieroglyphic symbols function both phonetically and logographically, depending on context. The boundaries are not hard and fast: hieroglyphs do not maintain caste distinctions.

sign	transliteration	identification	phonetic value
𓅐	ꜣ	vulture	a (glottal stop preceding an **a**) aleph
𓇋	i	reed	i, y (Semitic yodh)
𓂝	ꜥ	forearm	guttural unknown to English, ꜥayin, a as in 'father'
𓅱	w	quail chick	w
𓃀	b	leg and foot	b
𓊪	p	stool	p
𓆑	j	horned viper	f
𓅓	m	owl	m
𓈖	n	water	n
𓂋	r	mouth	r
𓉔	h	reed shelter	h, as in 'house'
𓎛	ḥ	twisted fibres	emphatic h, as in 'ha!'
𓎛	ẖ	sieve	soft **ch**, as in Scottish 'loch'
𓄡	ḫ	animal belly	hard **ch**, as in German 'ich'

sign	transliteration	identification	value
—∞— or ⌠	s	door bolt/ folded cloth	s
▭	š	lake	**sh**
◿	ḳ	hill	emphatic k
◡	k	basket	k
⌷	g	pot stand	g
◠	t	loaf or bread	t
⬭	ṯ	hobble	**tj** or **ch**
⬭	d	hand	d
⌐	ḏ	snake	**dj**

23. The 24-letter Egyptian hieroglyphic 'alphabet' – a construct of Egyptologists, not the Egyptians – is in fact a consonantal signary. See the text for a fuller explanation

Moreover with pictograms, the picture does not necessarily give the meaning of the sign. A particular pictogram may act as a logogram in one phrase and a phonetic sign in another (the rebus principle). To give one of the simpler examples, the 'child' pictogram 𓀔 can act either as a determinative (logogram) for 'child' or as a biconsonantal phonetic sign for *nn*. This ambiguity may give headaches to decipherers and Egyptologists, but it is also part of the fascination of reading hieroglyphic.

Coptic	name	phonetic value
ⲁ	alpha	a
Ⲃ	vita	v (b)
Ⲅ	gamma	g
Ⲇ	delta	d
Ⲉ	epsilon	e
Ⲍ	zita	z
Ⲏ	ita	i, e
Ⲑ	tita	t
Ⲓ	iota	i
Ⲕ	kappa	k
ⲗ	laula	l
Ⲙ	mi	m
Ⲛ	ni	n
Ⲝ	xi	x
Ⲟ	omicron	o
Ⲡ	pi	p
Ⲣ	ro	r
Ⲥ	sima	s
Ⲧ	tau	t
Ⲩ	ypsilon	y, u
Ⲫ	phi	ph
Ⲭ	khi	ch, kh
Ⲯ	psi	ps
Ⲱ	omega	o
Ⲳ	shei	s
Ϥ	fai	f
Ϩ	hori	h
Ϫ	djandja	g
Ϭ	chima	c
Ϯ	ti	ti

24. The 30-letter Coptic alphabet is based on the Greek alphabet with the addition of six extra signs

With these caveats, hieroglyphs may be classified as follows: a. uniconsonantal signs, b. biconsonantal signs, c. triconsonantal signs, d. phonetic complements, and e. determinatives/logograms.

There are some 24 uniconsonantal signs (depending on how variants are counted), some of which appear in the cartouches of Alexander, Cleopatra, Ptolemy, and Ramesses, as discovered by Young and Champollion. The uniconsonantal signs are often referred to as an 'alphabet', despite their not including true vowels and despite the fact that their usage is not distinct from that of other kinds of hieroglyphic phonetic sign. The table on pages 83–84 shows the so-called hieroglyphic 'alphabet', as constructed by Egyptologists, though unknown to the ancient Egyptians. Every sign is pictographic. The first three sounds in the table are vowels in English but consonants in Egyptian.

It is instructive to compare the hieroglyphic 'alphabet' with the 30 signs of the Coptic alphabet (page 85), a true alphabet used to write the latest stage of ancient Egyptian, which flourished from the 4th century AD. In its standard (Sahidic) form, the Coptic alphabet consists of the 24 letters of the Greek alphabet plus six signs borrowed from the Egyptian demotic script, which stand for Coptic sounds not symbolized in the Greek alphabet. Vowels are represented, and no letter is pictographic, unlike hieroglyphic.

Here are some of the biconsonantal and triconsonantal hieroglyphs:

Biconsonantal signs

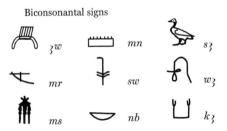

Triconsonantal signs

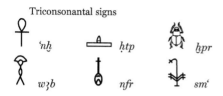

'Phonetic complementing' means the addition of a uniconsonantal sign (or signs) to a word to emphasize or confirm its pronunciation. There is no equivalent in writing English, though we might imagine adding a special vowel sign (as found in the International Phonetic Alphabet) to 'bow' – so as to distinguish 'bow [and arrow]' from 'bow [one's head]'. With hieroglyphic, the usual phonetic complement is a single sign reiterating the final consonant of the main sign. Some examples are highlighted:

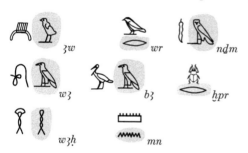

But it is common to add two or even three phonetic complements:

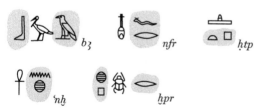

'Determinatives' are logograms added to the end of phonetic signs to indicate a word's meaning, and to discriminate where two or more meanings are possible. The cartouche is also a sort of determinative (as is the capital letter used in English to mark a proper name). Many determinatives are clearly pictographic, as highlighted here:

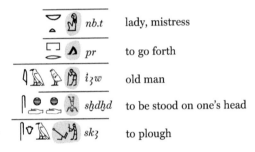

	nb.t	lady, mistress
	pr	to go forth
	iȝw	old man
	sḥdḥd	to be stood on one's head
	skȝ	to plough

The 'striking man' determinative shown in the last word is used, too, in the words for 'education' and 'taxes'! It determines words that involve forceful activity or action of some kind.

An exquisite example of determinatives is provided by the word *wn*, which consists of a biconsonantal sign ![sign] and a phonetic complement ∿∿∿, that may be combined with the following six determinatives, shown highlighted:

open
determinative: door

hurry
determinative: running legs

mistake
determinative: evil bird

become bald
determinative: lock of hair

Hermopolis
determinative: crossed roads

light
determinative: sun with rays

Sometimes more than one determinative is used:

cut open
determinatives:
knife, force

fugitives
determinatives: legs, man, plural

The cartouche of Tutankhamun on page 91, from the upper part of an inlaid box found in his tomb, demonstrates the logoconsonantal fundamentals of hieroglyphic writing. We can read it from the top.

∮ The single reed is a uniconsonantal sign with approximate value *i* (a vowel in English but a weak consonant in Egyptian).

⊏⊐ The game board with playing pieces is a biconsonantal sign with value *mn*.

∿ Water is a uniconsonantal sign with value *n*. Functioning (as here) as a phonetic complement, it reinforces the sound of *n* in *mn*.

These three signs are therefore read *imn*, which is normally pronounced *imen* or, more commonly, *amon* or *amun*. (Vowels are of course mostly absent in hieroglyphic spelling.) Amun was the god of Thebes (modern Luxor), regarded as the king of the gods during the New Kingdom, when Tutankhamun ruled. Out of respect, his name is placed first.

⌒ The half circle is a uniconsonantal sign with value *t*. It appears twice in the cartouche.

The quail chick is a uniconsonantal sign with value *w*, a weak consonant similar to the vowel *u*.

☥ This is the triconsonantal 'ankh' sign meaning 'life' or 'living' (which later became the 'handled or eyed' cross, *crux ansata*, of the Coptic church).

These four signs therefore read 'tutankh'.

The shepherd's crook is a logogram meaning 'ruler'.

The column is a logogram for Heliopolis, a city near Cairo.

This is the heraldic plant of Upper Egypt. It is a logogram for Upper Egypt.

'Heliopolis of Upper Egypt' is another name for the city of Thebes. So the complete cartouche reads: 'Tutankhamun, Ruler of Thebes'.

Egyptian hieroglyphic inscriptions have been described as 'boasting made permanent'. But at their finest, they also exert a mysterious charm exceeding that of all other ancient scripts. The skilful integration of hieroglyphs with the objects they adorn is a quintessential feature of ancient Egyptian writing. Another of the objects belonging to Tutankhamun is a wooden mirror case covered in gold and shaped in the form of an 'ankh'. The 'ankh' is both a hieroglyph and a symbol of life itself.

25. This cartouche of Tutankhamun demonstrates that Egyptian hieroglyphic is a logoconsonantal script. See the text for a fuller explanation

Chapter 6
Alphabets

If the emergence of writing is full of riddles, the enigma of the first alphabet is even more perplexing. That the alphabet reached the modern world via the ancient Greeks is generally known, given that 'alphabet' derives from the first two of the Greek letters, alpha and beta. That said, specialists have no clear idea of how and when the alphabet appeared in Greece, some four centuries after the disappearance of the syllabic Linear B around 1200 BC; how the Greeks thought of adding letters standing for vowels as well as the consonants of the Phoenician script; and how, even more fundamentally, the idea of an alphabet occurred to the pre-Greek societies at the eastern end of the Mediterranean during the 2nd millennium BC. Scholars have devoted their lives to these questions, but the evidence is too scanty for firm conclusions.

Did the alphabetic principle somehow evolve from the syllabic, logosyllabic, and logoconsonantal scripts of Mesopotamia, Egypt, Anatolia, and Crete – or did it strike a single unknown individual in a 'flash'? And why was an alphabet thought necessary? Was it the result of commercial imperatives, as seems most likely? In other words, did business require a simpler and quicker means of recording transactions than, say, Babylonian cuneiform or Egyptian hieratic, and also a convenient way to write the babel of languages of the various empires, tribes, and groups trading with each other in the eastern Mediterranean during the 2nd millennium BC? If so, then it is surprising that there is absolutely no evidence of trade and commerce in the early alphabetic inscriptions of Greece (unlike in the Linear B tablets). This and other considerations have led a few scholars such as Barry Powell, in his controversial book *Homer and the Origin of the Greek Alphabet*, to postulate that the Greek alphabet was invented in the 8th century BC in order to write down the orally preserved epics of Homer.

In the absence of proof, anecdote and myth have filled the vacuum. Children have often been invoked as inventors of the alphabet, because they would not have invested effort in learning the existing scripts of adults – particularly those adult scribes who had undergone a gruelling training in cuneiform or hieroglyphic. One possibility is that a bright Canaanite child in what is now northern Syria, fed up with having to learn cuneiform, took the uniconsonantal idea from Egyptian hieroglyphic and invented some new signs for the basic consonantal signs of his own Semitic language. Perhaps he doodled them first in the dust of some ancient street in Canaan: a simple outline of a house, 'beth' (the 'bet' in 'alphabet'), became the sign for 'b'. In the 20th century, Rudyard Kipling's cave-dwelling child protagonist Taffimai in the *Just So* story *How the Alphabet Was Made*, designs what she calls 'noise-pictures'. The letter A is a picture of a carp with its mouth wide open and its fishy barbel hanging down like the cross-bar of 'A'; this, Taffy tells her father, looks like his open mouth when he utters the sound *ah*. The letter S represents a snake, and stands for the hissing sound of the snake. In this somewhat far-fetched way, a whole phonetic alphabet is invented by Taffimai.

The earliest alphabetic inscriptions

In *Jerusalem*, the poet William Blake wrote: 'God . . . in mysterious Sinai's awful cave/ To Man the wond'rous art of writing gave.' A small sphinx in the British Museum once seemed to show that Blake was right, at least about the origin of the alphabet. The sphinx was found in 1905 at Serabit el-Khadim in Sinai, a desolate place remote from civilization, by the Egyptologist Flinders Petrie. He was excavating some old turquoise mines that were active in ancient Egyptian times. Petrie dated the sphinx to the middle of the 18th dynasty (the dynasty of Tutankhamun); nowadays its date is thought to be about 1500 BC. On one side of it is a strange inscription. On the other, and between the paws, there are further inscriptions of the same kind, plus some Egyptian hieroglyphs that read: 'beloved of Hathor, mistress of turquoise'.

There were other similar unfamiliar inscriptions written on the rocks of this remote area. Petrie guessed that the script was probably an alphabet, because its signary appeared to have less than 30 signs; and he thought that its language was probably Semitic, since he knew that Semites from Canaan – modern Israel and Lebanon – had worked these mines for the pharaohs, in many cases as slaves.

Ten years later, another Egyptologist Alan Gardiner studied these 'proto-Sinaitic' signs and noted resemblances between some of them and certain pictographic Egyptian hieroglyphs. Gardiner decided to name each proto-Sinaitic sign with the Semitic word equivalent to the sign's meaning in Egyptian (the Semitic words were known from biblical scholarship). Thus the sign that resembled the Egyptian 'ox' hieroglyph Gardiner named with the Semitic word for 'ox' – 'aleph'. The sign resembling the Egyptian 'house' hieroglyph he dubbed 'beth'. The sign resembling the 'throwstick' hieroglyph he dubbed 'gimel', and the sign resembling the 'door' hieroglyph he dubbed 'daleth'. These four Semitic names are the same as the names of the first four letters of the Hebrew alphabet – a fact that did not surprise Gardiner since he knew that the Hebrews had lived in Canaan in the late 2nd millennium BC. It began to look as if the proto-Sinaitic signs might be precursors of the Hebrew alphabet.

Gardiner's hypothesis enabled him to translate one of the inscriptions that occurred on the Sinai sphinx. In its English transcription, with the vowels spelt out (unlike in Hebrew and other Semitic scripts of this early period), he read the name 'Baalat'. This made sense: Baalat means 'the Lady' and is a recognized Semitic name for the Egyptian goddess Hathor in the Sinai region. So the inscriptions on the sphinx seemed to be an Egyptian-Semitic bilingual. Unfortunately, no further decipherment proved tenable, mainly because of lack of inscriptions and the fact that many of the proto-Sinaitic signs had no hieroglyphic equivalents. Scholarly hopes of finding the biblical story of the Exodus in these Sinaitic scratchings were scotched. Nevertheless, it is conceivable that a script similar to the proto-Sinaitic script was used by Moses to write down the Ten Commandments on tablets of stone.

We still do not know if Gardiner's 1916 guess is correct, plausible though it is. For some decades after Petrie's discoveries in Sinai, the inscriptions were taken to be the 'missing link' between Egyptian hieroglyphic and the Phoenician (alphabetic) script of the 11th century BC. But why should lowly and enslaved miners in out-of-the-way Sinai have created an alphabet? *Prima facie*, they seem to be unlikely inventors. Subsequent discoveries in Lebanon and Israel, of a small number of fragmentary, quasi-pictographic, undeciphered proto-Canaanite inscriptions believed to predate the proto-Sinaitic inscriptions by a century or two, showed the Sinaitic theory of the alphabet to be a romantic fiction. These suggested that Canaanites were the inventors of the alphabet, which would be reasonable. They were cosmopolitan traders at the crossroads of the Egyptian, Hittite, Babylonian, and Cretan empires; they were not wedded to an existing writing system; they needed a script that was easy to learn, quick to write, and unambiguous. Although the idea was unproven, it seemed probable during the second half of the 20th century that the Canaanites created the first alphabet.

Recently, however, contrary evidence has appeared from Egypt itself. In 1999, two Egyptologists, John Coleman Darnell and his wife Deborah, made a discovery at Wadi el-Hol, west of Thebes, while they were surveying ancient travel routes. They found what appeared to be alphabetic writing dating from around 1900–1800 BC, a date considerably earlier than the proto-Canaanite inscriptions.

The two short inscriptions the Darnells found are written in a Semitic script, and according to the experts the primitive signs were most probably developed in a fashion similar to a semi-cursive form of the Egyptian script. The writer is thought to have been a scribe travelling with a group of mercenaries (there were many such mercenaries working for the pharaohs). If this theory turns out to be correct, then it looks as if the alphabetic idea was, after all, inspired by Egyptian hieroglyphic, but invented in Egypt, rather than Palestine – which would make the Darnells' theory a revised version of Gardiner's theory. Yet the new evidence is very far from conclusive, and the search for more inscriptions continues. The riddle of the alphabet's origin(s) – in Egypt, Palestine, Sinai, or perhaps somewhere else – has not yet been solved.

Alphabetic cuneiform

The earliest definite alphabet is the cuneiform alphabet from Ugarit, dating from the 14th century, later than the date of the proto-Canaanite and proto-Sinaitic inscriptions, which it in no sense visually resembles. Ancient Ugarit (modern Ras Shamra) lay on the coast in the northern part of Canaan. Its kingdom was a grand one by Canaanite standards. Its capital covered 52 acres and was heavily fortified. Large donkey caravans converged on the city from Syria, Mesopotamia, and Anatolia to exchange goods with merchants from Canaan and Egypt as well as the maritime traders who arrived by ship from Crete, Cyprus, and the Aegean. The city functioned as a great bazaar. Ten languages and five different scripts were used at Ugarit, which walked a political tightrope between the Egyptians and the Hittites; there are bilingual Ugaritic cuneiform-Hittite hieroglyphic inscriptions.

The dominant script of the kingdom appears to have been Akkadian cuneiform, at least to begin with. (Akkad was an important late-3rd-millennium kingdom of north-central Mesopotamia near Baghdad; Akkadian cuneiform predates the cuneiform used to write Babylonian and Assyrian, which were dialects of Akkadian.) But then someone in Ugarit, or some group – perhaps senior merchants? – decided, it seems, that Akkadian cuneiform was too cumbersome and unreliable a system for writing the city's native tongue. Instead, the idea of an alphabet was introduced, presumably imported from southern Canaan (the land of the proto-Canaanite inscriptions), though there is no evidence for this. Rather than adopting or adapting a small set of pictographic or quasi-pictographic signs, however, the people of Ugarit were conservative: they decided to write their new alphabet in cuneiform. The signs they invented, some 30 in all, bore no resemblance to the signs of Akkadian cuneiform – other than being wedge-shaped – just as the signs of Old Persian cuneiform invented under Darius bear no resemblance to those of Babylonian cuneiform.

Over 1,000 tablets in Ugaritic cuneiform have been discovered since 1929, and they were rapidly deciphered. They consist of administrative texts – commercial correspondence, tax accounts, and other governmental business records – written with 30 signs, and literary and religious texts written with only 27 signs. The latter bear striking similarities, in theme and even in phrasing, to stories from parts of the Old Testament. It seems that these biblical stories were written down many centuries before they were written in Hebrew.

How did the Ugaritic inventor(s) decide on the shapes of the signs and their order? Most likely the simplest signs were applied to the most frequently heard sounds. The order of the signs was probably adopted from that of the proto-Canaanite alphabet (the order of which is admittedly unknown). We can guess this from the fact that some of the Ugaritic tablets are 'abecedaries', that is, they list the signs in the cuneiform script in a fixed order that quite closely resembles the modern order (a, b, c, d, etc.) we use nearly 3,500 years later. Another tablet (broken), discovered only in 1955, goes even further. It lists the Ugaritic cuneiform signs in the same fixed order on the left and adds next to each sign its Akkadian cuneiform syllabic equivalent on the right. The tablet is in fact a school tablet: we can imagine some unfortunate child from Ugarit in the last centuries of the 2nd millennium BC labouring over the approximately 600 Akkadian signs and wondering why anyone should want to write in Akkadian script when a simple alphabetic alternative was available.

The Phoenician letters

There is no clear line of descent from the proto-Canaanite inscriptions of the first half of the 2nd millennium BC to the relatively stable, 22-letter alphabetic script written by the Phoenicians from about 1000 BC, the forerunner of the Hebrew script and the Greek alphabet. Ugarit and its cuneiform alphabet seem to have been wiped out around 1200 BC by the influx of the Sea Peoples. Another Canaanite experiment in creating a script took place on the coast south of Ugarit, at Byblos, some time during the 2nd millennium (the date is very uncertain). The Byblos script has been called 'pseudo-hieroglyphic', implying that it was influenced by Egyptian hieroglyphic. While this is quite possible, there is no certainty, and some of the signs resemble Linear A from Crete, an equally likely candidate as an influence. At any rate, the Byblos 'pseudo-hieroglyphs' are undeciphered; all that can be said for sure is there are about 120 distinct signs, and hence the script cannot be an alphabet. It seems to have had no effect on the subsequent Phoenician script.

Yet another early inscription from what is now Israel, an ostracon (inscribed potsherd) dating from about the 12th century BC, suggests that the alphabetic idea was catching on. It has more than 80 letters in five lines written by an unskilled hand, and appears to be a rather unsuccessful attempt by a semi-literate person at writing an abecedary, which after some letters degenerated into a collection of random signs without meaning.

The earliest recognizably Phoenician inscriptions come from Byblos. They date from the 11th century BC, and inaugurate a script that would continue to be written all around the Mediterranean for the next millennium and more. Its latest variant, found at Carthage, the Phoenician city on the coast of north Africa near modern Tunis, is known as the Punic script. Punic influenced the script of the ancient Libyans – there are Punic-Libyan bilingual inscriptions from the 2nd century – who were the progenitors of the Berbers, the current indigenous inhabitants of northern Africa. This Libyan script provided a prototype for Tifinagh, meaning 'characters', the alphabet used today by the Tuareg, a Berber tribe. (Most languages in Africa are written either in the Arabic script, like Swahili, or in the Roman alphabet, with a mere handful of other indigenous scripts, notably the 1820s Vai syllabary of Liberia.)

The Phoenicians were the ancient world's greatest traders, who set out from their city-states, such as Byblos, Sidon, and Tyre, explored the Mediterranean and the Atlantic coast and may even have circumnavigated Africa, more than 2,000 years before the Portuguese. Among their most important items of merchandise was the purple dye exuded by the 'murex' snail, indeed 'Phoenician' is a Greek word (first used in Homer's *Iliad*), thought to mean 'dealer in purple'. We do not know a great deal about the Phoenicians, compared with the ancient Egyptians and Greeks, because they left few records and almost no literature, but we can tell from their inscriptions that their script went with them wherever they ventured. The names of their 22 letters – which

begin with 'aleph', 'beth', 'gimel', and 'daleth' – were the same as
those used by the Hebrews and in today's Hebrew script. The
Phoenicians indicated no vowels, only consonants. If we apply
their venerable alphabet to one of the earliest Phoenician
inscriptions – inscribed in the 11th century on the impressive
sarcophagus of King Ahiram of Byblos – we receive the following
somewhat sinister warning: 'Beware! Behold [there is] disaster for
you down here.'

The family of alphabets

From its unclear origins, probably among the Canaanites,
writing employing the alphabetic principle spread. It moved
westwards, via Greek and Etruscan, to the Romans and thence
to modern Europe; eastwards, via Aramaic in all probability, to
India and thence to Southeast Asia – assuming that we regard
the Indian scripts as alphabets (a classification we have already
questioned). By the 20th century, as a consequence of the
colonial empires, most of the world's peoples except the
Chinese and Japanese were writing in alphabetic scripts. The
majority of alphabets use between 20 and 40 basic signs, as
mentioned earlier, but a few have less and several have more
than these figures. Rotokas, the alphabet of a language spoken
by about 4,000 people on the island of Bougainville in Papua
New Guinea, has only 12 letters. The Khmer alphabet of
Cambodia used at Angkor Wat, a script of Indian origin, has
perhaps 74 signs, of which 33 are consonant symbols, the rest
being part of an unusually complex vowel system.

The Etruscans, who passed the Greek alphabet to the Romans,
inscribed many objects with their alphabet. One striking example,
a black vase or inkwell in the shape of a striding rooster inscribed
with a white alphabet, dates from the late 7th century BC. In
Mesopotamia, by the 5th century BC, many cuneiform documents
carried a notation of their substance in the Aramaic alphabet,

inked onto the clay tablet with a brush. From the time of Alexander the Great, cuneiform and Egyptian hieroglyphic were increasingly superseded by the Aramaic and Greek alphabets. In Egypt, by the 4th century AD, the Coptic alphabet had supplanted hieroglyphic and demotic.

The time chart below shows how some key modern alphabetic scripts emerged from the proto-Sinaitic/Canaanite scripts. It does not include the Indian scripts, since their connection with Aramaic is problematic and, strictly speaking, only partially proven. Nor does it show later alphabetic scripts such as the Cyrillic alphabet, the Korean Hangul alphabet or the Tifinagh alphabet of the Tuareg. It also omits the carved runes of northern Europe (especially Scandinavia) and the oghams of ancient Scotland and Ireland, since their origins are not known, although the runic alphabet, which dates from the 2nd century AD or earlier, was clearly influenced by the Roman alphabet. Lastly, it omits the so-called Cherokee 'alphabet', invented in the United States in 1821 by the Cherokee warrior Sequoyah. This remarkable system, with 86 signs, is really a syllabary, not an alphabet, based largely on assigning syllabic values to the individual letters of the Roman alphabet.

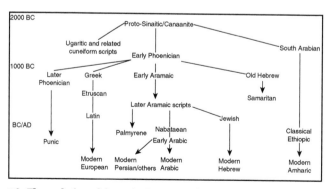

26. The evolution of the main European alphabetic scripts is well established, except for the origins of the alphabet in the first half of the 2nd millennium BC. The time-scale shown here is approximate

27. This playful cover for a Bengali children's magazine was designed
in 1988 by the film director Satyajit Ray, who was also a well-known
graphic designer, illustrator, and novelist. The magazine's title is
Sandesh, a Bengali word meaning both 'Sweetmeat' and 'News'. The
head/trunk of the elephant form the Bengali consonant 's', which has
an inherent vowel 'a'; the front of the body plus the second and third
legs form the conjunct Bengali consonant 'nd' (made from the signs for
'n' and 'd'); the first leg is the vowel 'e', in the form of a diacritic
preceding the conjunct; the back of the body and the fourth leg form
the Bengali consonant 'sh'. Modern Indian scripts, though often referred to as alphabets, are really an unusual fusion of alphabet and
syllabary

The Greeks and the alphabet

The Greek historian Herodotus called the alphabet 'phoinikeia grammata', 'Phoenician letters'; they were brought to Greece, he said, by the legendary Kadmos. Some 2500 years later, we are not much further forward in accounting for the origin of the Greek alphabet. Every scholar agrees that the Greeks borrowed the alphabet from the Phoenicians, but most now think this occurred among Greeks living in Phoenicia (a region of Canaan), from where it spread to the mother country.

We can perhaps visualize a Greek merchant sitting with a Phoenician teacher and copying down the signs and sounds, as the Phoenician pronounced each sign. The scope for distortion was considerable, because the 'barbarous' Phoenician letter names would not have rolled naturally off the Greek tongue. Consider how the untrained English ear cannot distinguish between 'rue' (street) and 'roux' (reddish) in French. Every language offers many similar examples. (Diego de Landa's Mayan 'alphabet' is a good one.) So, Phoenician 'aleph' (ox) became 'alpha' in Greek, 'beth' (house) became 'beta', 'gimel' (throwstick) became 'gamma', and so on. In the process, the names became meaningless (as they have in 'alphabet'). The 22 Phoenician consonants were adopted as Greek consonants *and* vowels, and a few new signs were added, which vary from place to place in Greece, creating several varieties of Greek alphabet. Although the introduction of vowels appears to be a major innovation, it seems to have occurred not because the Greek adapter intended it but because he could find no other way of transferring a particular Phoenician consonant into Greek. The consonants in question are 'weak', sometimes known as semivowels. Thus 'aleph', the weak consonantal glottal stop pronounced like a coughed *ah*, sounded to Greek ears like a funny way of saying *a*.

There are two major difficulties in deciding the date of invention of the Greek alphabet. First, the earliest known mainland alphabetic

Phoenician	Name	Phonetic value	Early Greek	Classical Greek	Name
𐤀	aleph	'	A	A	alpha
𐤁	beth	b	B	B	beta
𐤂	gimel	g	𐌂	Γ	gamma
𐤃	daleth	d	Δ	Δ	delta
𐤄	he	h	𐌄	E	epsilon
𐤅	waw	w	𐌅		digamma
𐤆	zayin	z	I	Z	zeta
𐤇	ḥeth	ḥ	𐌇	H	eta
𐤈	teth	ṭ	⊗	θ	theta
𐤉	yod	y	𐌉	I	iota
𐤊	kaph	k	𐌊	K	kappa
𐤋	lamed	l	𐌋	Λ	lambda
𐤌	mem	m	𐌌	M	mu
𐤍	nun	n	𐌍	N	nu
𐤎	samekh	s			xi
𐤏	ayin	'	O	O	omicron
𐤐	pe	p	𐌐	Π	pi
𐤑	sade	ṣ	M		san
𐤒	qoph	q	φ		qoppa
𐤓	reš	r	𐌓	P	rho
𐤔	šin	sh/s	𐌔	Σ	sigma
𐤕	taw	t	X		tau
				Y	upsilon
				X	chi
				Ω	omega

28. The Greeks borrowed their letter forms and many of the names of their letters from the established Phoenician script, for example 'alpha'/'aleph', 'kappa'/'kaph'

inscription dates from only around 730 BC. Second, there are no known practical or business documents for over 200 years after the appearance of the alphabet.

Before the decipherment of Linear B in 1952, the Greeks were regarded as illiterate until the arrival of the alphabet. Since the decipherment, it has been conventional to imagine a 'Dark Age' of illiteracy in Greece between the fall of the Homeric Greeks and the rise of the classical Greeks after, say, 800 BC. This is still the orthodox view. Some scholars, however, believe that the Dark Age is a fiction, and that the Greeks had knowledge of alphabetic writing much earlier than the 8th century BC, perhaps as early as 1100 BC. A principal piece of evidence in favour of this theory is that the direction of early Greek inscriptions is unstable: sometimes they run from right to left, sometimes from left to right, sometimes boustrophedon. But the direction of Phoenician writing, itself unstable prior to about 1050 BC, *was* stable, from right to left, probably by 800 BC. So, the argument goes, the Greeks must have borrowed the Phoenician script in the earlier phase of its development, not after it had settled down.

The date of the invention – anywhere between 1100 and 800 BC – is therefore controversial. The issue is likely to be resolved only by the discovery of Greek alphabetic inscriptions prior to the 8th century BC (as happened with Linear B at Knossos in 1900).

Even more controversial is *why* the alphabetic script suddenly appeared. It is certainly extraordinary that there are no economic documents at all among the early Greek inscriptions. Instead the early alphabet users from all parts of Greece display private, almost literary concerns; the above-mentioned inscription of 730 BC, written on a vase, which was probably a prize, refers to 'him who dances most delicately'. If economic inscriptions once existed on impermanent materials and simply perished, why does no trace of them remain, not even on potsherds?

One solution to the conundrum, seriously considered, is that the inventor of the alphabet was a brilliant contemporary of Homer who was inspired to record his epics. The vowelless Phoenician system proved useless for the task of writing epic verse, so a new writing system with vowels and rhythmic subtlety was needed. Though there are good grounds for this theory, it is surely likely that knowledge of such a feat would have been preserved by the Greeks themselves. But – sad to say for romantics – there is no hint in Greek tradition that Homer and the origin of the alphabet are connected.

The Greek and Latin letters

There was more than one alphabet in ancient Greece, as already mentioned. The alphabetic signs of classical Greece, which are still in use in Greece, are known as the Ionian alphabet. They did not become compulsory in Athenian documents until 403–402 BC. Long before this, Greek colonists had taken a somewhat different script, the Euboean alphabet, to Italy. This was the alphabet taken over by the Etruscans, with some modifications, and then adopted by the Romans.

The reason why modern European and modern Greek letter forms differ can therefore be traced to the use of the Euboean alphabet in Italy from around 750 BC. For instance, the letters A and B descend from the same signs in both the Euboean and Ionian alphabets, while C and D descend from the Euboean forms ⊂ and ▷, which differ from the Ionian forms preserved in the modern Greek letters Γ and Δ.

As an example of Etruscan and Roman modification, consider the Euboean gamma. Etruscan had no need of a sign for the voiced stop g, and so ⊂ took the phonetic value k. This meant that *three* Etruscan signs were used to write k (as in English 'think'): one sign before a (ka), a second sign before e and i (ce, ci), a third before u (qu). Latin spelling initially adopted this system, but since the

Latin language (unlike Etruscan) did have the voiced stop *g*, the early Latin letter 'C' could be pronounced either as *k* (as in Caesar pronounced *Kaisar*) or as *g* (as in Caius pronounced *Gaius*); later, the Romans introduced a new letter G, to disambiguate this phonetic distinction.

The Roman/Latin script was modified slightly in turn, on the way to becoming its modern English equivalent. There were four sounds in Anglo-Saxon for which there were no counterparts in Latin:

1. /w/ came to be written with a runic symbol Ᵽ known as wynn. In Middle English, this was replaced by 'uu' or 'w'; it is rarely found after 1300.

2. /θ/ and /ð/ – as in modern English 'thin' and 'this' – came to be written by a runic symbol known as 'thorn', þ. To this was later added the symbol ð, which was called 'eth'. In Middle English both letters were replaced by 'th'. But þ has survived in the 'Y' (standing for 'Th') of the artificial modern form 'Ye Olde English Tea Shoppe'.

3. /a/ – as in modern English 'hat' – was represented using the Latin digraph æ, which came to be called 'ash', after the name of the runic symbol representing the same sound. In Middle English this too had fallen out of use, probably as a result of sound changes.

In Eastern Europe, the Cyrillic alphabet, today used to write Russian, became the script for more than 60 languages. It originally had 43 letters, the majority of which appear to have been derived from the Greek scripts of the time. Its inventor was alleged to be St Cyril (c. 827–69), who was entrusted with the mission by the Byzantine emperor Constantine at the request of the Slav king of Moravia; the king wanted a script that was independent of the Roman church, which recognized only the Hebrew, Greek, and Latin scripts for the Bible. This is the legend. In fact, Cyril seems to have devised the Glagolitic alphabet; the Cyrillic script was created later. Cyrillic eventually replaced Glagolitic in the 12th century.

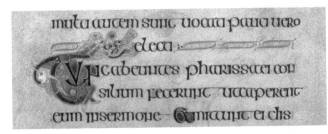

29. This detail is from the Book of Kells, which dates from before AD 807. Kept at Trinity College Library, Dublin, the manuscript records the Gospels in the so-called Insular script developed by Irish monks from the uncial script used in official Roman documents of the 3rd century AD onwards (Latin '*litterae unciales*' means 'inch-high letters'). Each monastery developed its own characteristic variant of uncials

Runes

From as far back as the 2nd century AD, runic symbols carved in stone, metal, and wood were used to record the early stages of the languages Gothic, Danish, Swedish, Norwegian, English, Frisian, and Frankish, and the various tribal tongues of central Germania. These peoples were therefore not illiterate, as sometimes thought, before the period when they became Christian and began to use the Roman alphabet.

We do not know where and when runes were invented. Finds of early rune-inscribed objects in Eastern Europe, at Pietroassa in Romania, Dahmsdorf in central Germany, and Kowel in Russia, indicates that runes may have been invented in that general area, perhaps by Goths on the Danube frontier or beside the River Vistula. Another hypothesis notes the resemblance between the runes and characters used in the inscriptions of the Alpine valleys of southern Switzerland and northern Italy and goes on to ascribe the invention to Romanized Germani from that area. A third hypothesis prefers one of the Germanic tribes of Denmark, perhaps southern Jutland, as the progenitors of runes; many of the earliest inscriptions come from this general area, and early runic texts continue to be found in various regions of Denmark. But on one point all scholars of runes agree: the Roman alphabet exercised influence of some kind on the runic script.

The runic alphabet has 24 letters, arranged in a peculiar order known as the 'futhark' after its first six letters. The script can be written from left to right, right to left, or even boustrophedon, in the early period. An individual letter could also be reversed on occasions, apparently at whim, and might even be inverted. There was no distinction between capital and lower-case letters.

Some of the runic letters are obviously related to the letters of the Roman alphabet 'R', 'I', and 'B'. Others could well be adaptations of Roman letters, notably 'F', 'U' (Roman V inverted), 'K' (Roman C), 'H', 'S', 'T', 'L' (Roman L inverted). But other runes, such as those representing g, w, j, and p, scarcely resemble Roman forms with the same phonetic value.

Even though runic inscriptions can usually be 'read' – in the same sense as Etruscan inscriptions – their meaning is frequently cryptic, because of our lack of knowledge of the early Germanic languages. Hence the origin of the English expression 'to read the runes' – meaning to make an educated guess on the basis of scanty and ambiguous evidence. As a scholar of runes, R. I. Page, has ironically remarked, the First Law of Runodynamics is 'that for every inscription there shall be as many interpretations as there are scholars working on it.'

Chapter 7
Chinese and Japanese writing

To understand the scripts of East Asia, we need to begin with the languages of China. What the world beyond China calls the Chinese language is in fact made up of eight regional languages ('topolects' or 'regionalects' in linguistic parlance) that are mutually unintelligible, and tens, if not hundreds, of true dialects. Over 70 per cent of Chinese do however speak a single language, known by various names: Mandarin (the most familiar name outside China), Putonghua ('common speech'), Guoyu ('national language'), and Standard Modern Chinese. These are not entirely equivalent terms, but the essential point is that modern *written* Chinese is based on this single language. It is the dominance of Mandarin speakers in China, both in classical times and today, which has fuelled the myth of the universal intelligibility of Chinese characters, known as 'hanzi' in Mandarin. According to this long-standing yet false notion, all language speakers who use, or have in the past used, a hanzi-based script, such as the Cantonese, Japanese, Koreans, and Vietnamese, can understand each other in writing, even though their languages differ vastly from Mandarin.

Chinese belongs to the Sino-Tibetan family of languages, which may be loosely compared to the Indo-European family. The various Chinese regionalects such as Yue (Cantonese) and Wu (spoken in the Shanghai region) are then analogous to English, Dutch, and German in the Germanic group or French, Spanish, and Italian in the Romance group; while the dialects within Mandarin, such as those spoken in Beijing and Nanking, are comparable to the British, American, and Australian dialects of English or the Neapolitan, Roman, and Tuscan dialects of Italian. Just as speakers of English and speakers of German cannot understand each other's literature without learning each other's language (despite sharing the same Roman script), so Cantonese speakers cannot understand modern written Chinese properly without learning how to speak Mandarin. Cantonese is nearer to Mandarin than, say, Spanish is to French, but the differences in grammar, vocabulary, and pronunciation are still major ones.

For example, there are six tones in Cantonese and only four tones in Mandarin: high level, high rising, low dipping, and high falling. (And Japanese has no tones at all of the Chinese kind.) Tones in Chinese disambiguate the large number of words that would otherwise be homophonous; when, as often happens, foreigners ignore tones, they naturally conclude that Chinese is an even more 'difficult' language than it really is. Thus, 'ma', without indication of tone, can mean 'mother', 'hemp', 'horse', or 'scold'; 'shuxue' can mean 'mathematics' or 'blood transfusion'; 'guojiang' can mean 'you flatter me' or 'fruit paste'. With tone indication the different meanings are clearly distinguished. In writing, instead of tones, the distinction is generally made by combining different characters with one character of the same phonetic value, to make a new character.

Classifying characters

How can the many thousands of Chinese characters be analysed and classified for the purpose of, say, dictionary making? There is no simple answer. Traditionally, characters have been divided into five (some would argue six) groups according to the principle of their composition.

The first group consists of pictographic logograms, such as those found on the ancient oracle bones. The second group represents words not pictorially but with other visually logical logograms. For example, the numbers one, two, three are represented by one, two, and three lines. Another example is:

above   below

We might call this group 'simple representational'.

In the third group, which might be called 'compound representational', the logic is more complex: at the level of ideas rather than the visual. A favourite example is the combination of the characters for sun and moon to form 'bright':

日   月   明

sun   moon   bright

The fourth group involves the rebus principle. On page 33, the character for wheat is used for 'come', because the word for wheat, 'lái', is homophonous with the Chinese word for 'come'. Another example is the character for 'elephant' that is also used for 'image', because both words are pronounced *xiàng*.

The final group, often termed 'semantic-phonetic', involves the combination of a character indicating the meaning of a word with a character indicating its pronunciation. Thus the semantic character for 'female person' is combined with the character having the phonetic value *mǎ* to create a new character meaning 'mother':

'female person' +   *mǎ*   =   'mā' (mother)

Note that the phonetic component does not give the pronunciation precisely: the tones differ. The difference is crucial, given that 'mǎ' means 'horse'.

It is often imagined that the meaning 'mother' is really derived from the combination of two ideas, with no phonetic element involved. In other words, woman + horse = mother ('female horse') – rather than its being derived from the combination of one idea with a phonetic symbol. But this 'ideographic' explanation, appealing as it is (not least to overworked mothers), has no foundation and is a good example of the misunderstandings of Chinese characters that abound. It is incorrect to think of Chinese characters as ideographic (or purely logographic) in this sense; there is always a phonetic element in Chinese writing.

The numbers of characters in the five groups have not remained constant with time. There was a higher proportion of pictographic characters during the Shang dynasty than is now the case. Today the vast majority of characters, over 90 per cent, are of the 'semantic-phonetic' variety.

To know that a Chinese word is pronounced and written in a certain way will not enable its meaning to be looked up in a Chinese dictionary. For the Chinese have not produced a single dictionary with entries arranged in simple alphabetical order – with, say, the character pronounced *xiàng* coming later in the dictionary than the character pronounced *mǎ* ('x' normally coming after 'm'). Instead they have contrived a host of other schemes based on characters' *shape*, rather than their pronunciation or meaning.

Some dictionaries arrange the characters by the number of strokes required to draw a particular character, a series of movements drummed into Chinese writers at school. It is common to see Chinese dictionary users counting up the number of strokes on their fingers. These could easily be 20 strokes or more. Where the number of strokes is miscounted, a time-consuming search is required in the general area of the nearest guess at the stroke number.

More popular is the 'radical-stroke' system, employed by the first Chinese dictionary, which was compiled in the 2nd century AD. This arranged its 9353 characters under 540 semantic keys or 'radicals', such as 'water', 'vegetation', 'insect'; the number of keys was later reduced to 214. The radicals were in turn ordered according to the number of strokes – from 1 to 17 – with a fixed order imposed on radicals having the same number of strokes. To use the dictionary, one had to determine under which radical the word in question might be classified – often a tricky decision. The radical in the character for 'mother' would probably be classified under 'female person'. One popular dictionary contained a 'List of Characters Having Obscure Radicals' that included fully one *twelfth* of its 7773 characters!

The radical-stroke system of 214 radicals remained standard until the 1950s. Now, with Simplified characters (introduced from 1955 onwards), dictionaries arrange the radicals under anything from 186 to 250 categories; there is no standard. The resultant chaos – as if, say, different Western dictionaries used different A–Z orderings – can easily be imagined.

The phonetic component of Chinese characters can be used to classify them, too – broadly speaking syllabically. Native Chinese speakers have generally left this approach to phonetically minded foreigners, who in the past were mainly missionaries. One of them, W. E. Soothill, classified some 4,300 characters on the basis of 895 phonetics during the 1880s.

Each column of the 'Soothill Syllabary' is headed by a phonetic, for example 'mǎ'. The pronunciation of the characters in a column closely follows this phonetic component; but in appearance and stroke number, not to mention meaning, the characters in a column differ enormously. If we choose some phonetic columns and then pick out characters that share a similar semantic component (radical), we can create a semantic-phonetic grid, with its columns classified by the same or similar phonetic component and its rows by similar semantic component.

In the column under phonetic component 264, 'áo', the phonetic is a good guide to the pronunciation of four characters, which are a combination of phonetic 264 with the semantic components 9 ('person'), 64 ('hand'), 75 ('wood'), and 85 ('water'): the four combined characters are pronounced 'áo' ('proud'), 'áo' ('shake'), 'āo' ('barge'), and 'áo' ('stream'). But if instead we follow a row of the grid, such as all characters having the semantic component 9 for 'person', the semantic component is *not* a good guide to meaning: semantic 9, combined with phonetics 264, 282, 391, and 597, gives four characters having no obvious connection with 'person' meaning 'proud', 'good', 'lucky', and 'help' (each pronounced very differently, of course). Generally, the phonetic component of a character provides a better guide to the pronunciation than the semantic component does to meaning – contrary to the predictions of scholars who maintain that Chinese is an essentially logographic (or 'ideographic') script in which phoneticism is hardly significant.

In practice, native speakers use both semantic and phonetic clues when reading characters. Consider these two characters that share the same phonetic component 丁:

A 仃 'dīng' ('alone')

B 氵丁 'tīng' ('sandspit')

The pronunciation of this phonetic component (phonetic 2 in the Soothill syllabary) is *dīng*. It represents the pronunciation of character A exactly and the pronunciation of character B with 75 per cent accuracy (three phonemes, *i*, *ng*, and tone, out of a possible total of four phonemes). The semantic component in each case is also relevant, though much less so than the phonetic: in A, 亻(semantic 9) suggests 'person' (compare 'alone'), in B 氵 (semantic 85) suggests 'water' (compare 'sandspit'). A Chinese reader could begin the process of guessing the meaning and pronunciation of these characters either with the phonetic or with the semantic components. But in either case, he or she would need to have *learnt* in advance the significance of the three components; their shapes alone would be of no practical assistance.

Thus, for a native speaker, the reading of Chinese characters is part memory feat and part ability to spot interconnections. What it certainly does not resemble – despite claims to the contrary – is either a highly sophisticated form of pictography, or the memorization and recall of several thousand telephone numbers.

30. **The scholar prepares to write in *The Four Joys of Nan Sheng-lu*, 1649, by Chen Hongshou. His paperweight is a carved lion; before him is a bowl of water with a ladling spoon, inkstick, and inkstone with ink ground in it; on his left is a jug of wine, a cup, and a citron in a bowl. The only item missing is his brush**

Chinese readers are not like the Chinese telegraph clerks of the recent past who did indeed convert each character into a standard four-digit code. (Using this code, 'arriving tomorrow noon' would be sent as 2494 1131 0022 0582 0451.) However intimidating Chinese characters may appear to the foreign learner, they are by no means entirely random.

Japanese writing

The Japanese language possibly belongs to the Altaic family (along with Mongolian and Turkish), and is probably related to Korean, but it is about as different from Chinese in phonological system, grammatical categories, and syntactic structures as two languages can be. Nevertheless, the Japanese based their writing system on Chinese characters, which they refer to as 'kanji', their approximation of the Mandarin 'hanzi'. In borrowing the characters, the Japanese altered the Mandarin pronunciation of kanji in particular ways corresponding to the sounds of Japanese.

Eventually, during the first half of the 1st millennium AD, the Japanese invented a fairly small set of supplementary phonetic symbols – which are actually simplified versions of the kanji – known as 'kana', in order to make clear how the Sino-Japanese kanji were to be pronounced and also how to transcribe native (Japanese) words. It would have been simpler, one might reasonably think, if the Japanese had used *only* these invented kana and had abandoned the Chinese characters altogether – but this would have entailed the rejection of a writing system of enormous prestige. Just as a knowledge of Latin was until recently a *sine qua non* for the educated European – as was a knowledge of the oldest Mesopotamian literary language Sumerian for those educated in Akkadian in the 2nd millennium BC – so a familiarity with Chinese has always been considered essential by the Japanese literati. This is still true in Japan, although the burden of reading kanji, combined with their relative unsuitability for computing,

31. *Kojiki*, the earliest work of Japanese literature, is written in Chinese characters (kanji), annotated with smaller Japanese phonetic symbols (kana). This copy was printed from woodblocks in 1803

has led to some decline in their status, as compared to kana and the Roman alphabet. (Hence the upsurge in popularity of the Japanese comics, 'manga', which contain relatively few kanji.)

Thus the earliest work of Japanese literature, *Kojiki*, an ancient history of Japan completed in AD 712, has the main text in kanji. Written beside these characters, however, are smaller Japanese kana, syllabic symbols indicating the Japanese pronunciation of each kanji.

Kana, kanji, and romaji

The kana come in two varieties, known today as 'hiragana' ('easy kana') and 'katakana' ('side kana'). Each consists of some 46 signs augmented by two special diacritics (not shown on page 120) and by a technique of symbol combination for representing complex syllables. Note that curved lines are relatively common in hiragana, while straight lines tend to be characteristic of katakana.

Why *two* syllabaries? Originally hiragana was used for informal writing and katakana for more formal works such as official documents, histories, and lexical works. Today hiragana is the more frequently employed script, and katakana serves roughly the same function as italic type in alphabetic scripts. Foreign terms and foreign names recently borrowed into Japanese are nearly always written in katakana. For example, 'French restaurant' is written with nine katakana as 'fu-ra-n-su-re-su-to-ra-n'; 'Clint Eastwood' as 'Ku-ri-n-to-I-su-to-u-tsu-do' (there being no *l* sound in Japanese).

An alternative for words of foreign origin is to use 'romaji', words written in the roman alphabet. During the 1980s, the Roman alphabet began to invade Japanese writing through advertising. Words that before would have been written in katakana in magazines and newspapers and on television and billboards suddenly began to be written in Roman letters, even in the middle

a	ka	sa	ta	na	ba	ma	ya	ra	wa	
あ	か	さ	た	な	は	ま	や	ら	わ	
ア	カ	サ	タ	ナ	ハ	マ	ヤ	ラ	ワ	
i	ki	sbi	cbi	ni	bi	mi		ri		
い	き	し	ち	に	ひ	み		り		
イ	キ	ツ	チ	ニ	ヒ	ミ		リ		
u	ku	su	tsu	nu	fu	mu	yu	ru		
う	く	す	つ	ぬ	ふ	む	ゆ	る		
ウ	ク	ス	ツ	ヌ	フ	ム	ユ	ル		
e	kesu	se	te	ne	be	me		re		
え	け	せ	て	ね	へ	め		れ		
エ	ケ	セ	テ	ネ	ヘ	メ		レ		
o	ko	so	to	no	bo	mo	yo	ro	(w)o	n
お	こ	そ	と	の	ほ	も	よ	ろ	を	ん
オ	コ	ソ	ト	ノ	ホ	モ	ヨ	ロ	ヲ	ン

32. **Japanese syllabic symbols, known as kana, come in two varieties: hiragana (top rows, highlighted) and katakana (bottom rows)**

of a sentence otherwise written in kana and kanji. As the head of product development at Sony remarked in 1984, the Roman word 'love' can be written on a kid's school bag, because it has a 'a kind of cuteness and charm', but the Chinese kanji for 'love' cannot be used: 'It would carry a feeling of intrinsic difficulty, create resistance instead of sales appeal.'

How do the Japanese decide whether to use kana or kanji in a sentence? There is a fair amount of fluctuation and overlap between the two. However, as a very general guide, kana serve to represent inflectional affixes, grammatical particles, many adverbs, and the vast majority of words of European origin, while kanji are employed to write the majority of nouns – both Japanese and Sino-Japanese ones, other than those of Western origin – and many verb and adjective bases.

All Japanese sentences can in principle be written entirely in kana. In fact one of the greatest works of Japanese literature – Murasaki Shikibu's *The Tale of Genji* of the early 11th century – was written in hiragana (though her original manuscript no longer exists). Kana writing was for centuries the main style of writing used by women. Today most Japanese Braille is written in kana, without using any kanji; and the result is that the Japanese blind are able to read more easily than many of the Japanese sighted!

Why then do most Japanese not convert to writing in kana alone, leaving the literati to relish kanji? Why do they persist with the awkward intricacies of the mixed kana-and-kanji script? One reason is that spelling out the kanji phonetically would make sentences much longer. Another is that there would be confusion between kana in adjacent words, since gaps between words are not used in writing Japanese. But perhaps the most compelling reason is that many words in Japanese have the same pronunciation (Chinese avoids this problem with tones), and would therefore take the same spelling in kana.

To explain this last point further, Japanese has homophony on a grand scale. For example, the word pronounced *kansho* has the following 17 meanings (at least): vice merchant, sentimental, interference, victory, irritable, to praise, to encourage, encouragement, to appreciate, to admire, contemplation, to observe the weather, atoll, buffer/bumper, government office, to expedite, to manage. Each meaning is distinguishable when written in kanji, but not in kana. Admittedly not all Japanese homophones are as wide-ranging as this one, and they would in many cases by clarified by the context of a word in a sentence. Nevertheless, homophony is widely thought to be a major barrier to kana-only writing. So the kanji persist.

Imagine that you have to spell your name and address over the telephone in Japanese. It is easy enough with an alphabet, well-nigh impossible with certain kanji that distinguish personal and place names sounding alike. How do you describe each of some 2,000 symbols? You have to speak of, say, 'three-stroke *kawa*' (*sanbonkawa*) – as opposed to all other kanji that can be read *kawa*; or *yoko-ichi*, the kanji read *ichi* that is written with a single horizontal stroke. But this method of naming kanji is of limited usefulness, because kanji shapes vary so widely and so uniformly.

Consequently, in face-to-face conversations, in the absence of pencil and paper (or the ubiquitous exchange of business cards), the Japanese resort to pantomime: they use the right index finger as a 'pencil' to 'write' the kanji in the air or on the palm of the left hand. But often this too fails, and a person must use an appropriate common word as a label for the kanji. For example, of the dozens of kanji that can be read *to*, only one can also stand for the noun '*higashi*' ('east'); this character is then readily labelled as *higashi to iu ji*, 'the character *higashi*'. When, however, a kanji has only one reading, and you wish to describe it, you have a problem. To identify the kanji that stands for *to* in 'sato' ('sugar'), you cannot do much more than to say something like, 'It's the one used in the last syllable of the word for sugar.' If that does not trigger the memory of the person you are talking to, you must go back to the shape: 'It's the kanji with the "rice" radical on the left, and the tang of "Tang dynasty" on the right.'

No wonder, then, that in 1928 George Sansom, an authority on Japan, remarked of its writing system: 'There is no doubt that it provides for a fascinating field of study, but as a practical instrument it is surely without inferiors.' A modern authority, J. Marshall Unger, added recently: 'In a broad sense, over the centuries, Japanese script has "worked". Japanese culture has not flourished *because of* the complexities of its writing system, but it has undeniably flourished in spite of them.'

Chapter 8
Scribes and materials

Writing is a skill that anyone can learn, but it is also a craft and even an art. The finest stone and papyrus hieroglyphic inscriptions from Egypt, the exquisite cuneiform cylinder-seal engravings in gemstones from Mesopotamia, the Chinese characters brushed on mulberry paper or incised into bronze, the gorgeously painted and annotated ceramics of the Maya, the calligraphic suras from the Koran carved into the marble façade of the Taj Mahal, the illuminated manuscripts of medieval Europe written on vellum, even the simply engraved wooden Rongorongo tablets of Easter Island – are all works of art. Until the mass education of the 20th century (and the arrival of the personal computer), every literate society had a class of professional scribes who were also artists.

'Scribes were held in the highest esteem among the ancient Maya, as they were in those other great calligraphic civilizations: ancient Egypt, China and Japan, Islam and Western Europe', writes Michael Coe in his magnificent book, *The Art of the Maya Scribe*, photographed by Justin Kerr.

> So highly were they regarded that they were recruited from the nobility and even from the royal house itself. Like other officials who directed the city-states ... during the Classic period, they wore their own distinctive costume and headdress, in which were prominently

displayed the tools of their profession—their brush pens and their carving tools. Even further, they often proudly signed their own works, their signatures appearing on relief sculptures ... and on fine decorated pottery, both painted and carved.

Among the most famous Mayan scribal works is the Dresden Codex, one of only four surviving 'books' of the ancient Maya. At the height of the Classic Maya civilization, AD 250 to 800, there were many such bark-paper codices with jaguar-skin covers, painted by scribes using brush or feather pens dipped in black or red paint held in conch-shell inkpots. But most of these codices were destroyed by the Spanish (such as Bishop de Landa) after their conquest of Mexico in the 16th century. The Dresden Codex is undated, but was probably painted just before the Spanish conquest and then taken to Europe by Hernan Cortés in the 1520s; in 1739, it was apparently purchased by the royal library of the court of Saxony in Dresden, the city where it remains today.

The codex consists of 39 leaves in a folding screen the size of a Michelin travel guide, which opens out to a length of 3.5 metres. On each leaf, which has been sized with a fine coat of lime, the scribe has painted with extreme care a series of gods and animals, often in many colours, accompanied by numerals and glyphs. (These glyphs proved to be of decisive help to the leading Mayan glyphic decipherer, Yuri Knorosov, in the 1950s.) In fact, eight scribes were involved, according to detailed study of the glyphs, which show the styles of eight different hands. So fine is the delineation of the numeral bars, the glyph interiors, and the deity figures that, according to Coe, the work was done with quill pens, either chisel-edged or with a very narrow tip – not with the more usual brush pens.

A unique 'codex-style' Mayan vase from the 8th century, a bit like an ancient comic, shows the scribes themselves. They are being taught by the scribal god Pawahtun. In one scene, two young male scribes, wearing on their heads what scholars call the 'stick bundle'

– probably blanks for quill pens – squat before the aged deity. The god gestures towards an open codex with a pen, while 'speaking' the book's mathematical contents (as in a cartoon speech bubble), in the form of bar-and-dot numerals. In a second scene, on the other side of the vase, the god is clearly annoyed with the two novices, who now look apprehensive. The second speech bubble from the deity consists of two glyphs. Using the syllabic system deciphered by Knorosov and others, we can read the glyphic ending as the word *tatab(i)*. In a 16th-century Mayan dictionary, the word *tataah* refers to careless and hasty writing!

Scribes in ancient Mesopotamia and Egypt

In ancient Mesopotamia scribes were trained in scribal schools. Boys, and a very few girls, practised on clay by copying a few lines of cuneiform written by a teacher: the names of gods, a list of technical terms, a brief fragment of literature or a proverb. Many such school tablets survive, with the teacher's version on one side and the pupil's less competent version on the other.

Once trained, scribes had many roles. The most influential scribes were those at the royal court and the personal secretaries of various city governors in the country. Others were attached to temples, still others to the textile industry, ship-building, pottery workshops, and transport services. Most were in agriculture, assisting in the maintenance of irrigation canals, registering the rations of the labour force and the storage of the harvest, and recording the supply and guarding of agricultural tools; they also dealt with the receipt and conveyance of animals. Finally, scribes filled positions in the field of law. Many were probably without real power, but some may have been equivalent to a modern 'secretary' of a major institution. However, scribes in Mesopotamia were definitely less revered than scribes in ancient Egypt and China.

33. In the late 8th century BC, two Assyrian warriors (left) greet each other after a battle; two scribes (centre) record the number slain. The scribe in the foreground writes in imperial Aramaic, an alphabetic script, using a brush on papyrus. His bearded colleague writes in the traditional cuneiform script on a clay or wax-covered tablet

Around 2000 BC, an anonymous school-teacher wrote an essay in cuneiform, 'Schooldays', which is one of the most human documents excavated in the Near East. In it, an alumnus of the scribal school, 'Old Grad', looks back nostalgically to his schooldays. 'My headmaster read my tablet, said: "There is something missing," caned me.' Then, one by one, just about everyone in authority finds an excuse to give a caning. And so 'I [began to] hate the scribal art, neglect the scribal art.' The boy goes home to his father in despair and asks him to invite his teacher home. The teacher comes, is given the chair of honour, is attended by his pupil, who thereupon unfolds to his father his knowledge of the scribal art. The father heartily praises the teacher, turns to his household servants and says: 'Make fragrant oil flow like water on his stomach and back; I want to dress him in a garment, give him some extra salary, put a ring on his hand.' The servants do as they are bidden and then the teacher speaks emolliently to the boy:

> Young fellow, [because] you hated not my words, neglected them not, may you complete the scribal art from beginning to end. Because you gave me everything without stint, paid me a salary larger than my efforts [deserve, and] have honoured me, may Nidaba, the queen of guardian angels, be your guardian angel, may your pointed stylus write well for you; may your exercises contain no faults.

In Egypt, we know less about the lives of scribes, because the evidence was written on papyrus (rarely on stone), and papyri do not last as well as clay tablets. Nevertheless it is clear from fragmentary papyri, and from surviving sculptures and writing implements and the prominence accorded to hieroglyphic inscriptions, that successful scribes were of high status. For example, a limestone statue of a scribe known as Kay, dating from around 2500 BC, excavated at Saqqara, shows him contentedly sitting cross-legged with a partially opened roll of papyrus on his lap. Another portrait of a scribe, in wood, from a slightly earlier period, shows Hesire, the chief of the royal scribes, standing regally with his writing implements clutched in his left hand. In Tutankhamun's tomb, there was a luxurious set of writing implements: an ivory palette, a gilded wood palette, an ivory and gold papyrus burnisher, and an elaborate pen case of gilded and inlaid wood.

The fragments of papyri contain moral advice reminiscent of that in the cuneiform tablets. A teacher writes to his pupil:

> I know that you frequently abandon your studies and whirl around in pleasure, that you wander from street to street and every house stinks of beer when you leave it . . . You, boy! You do not listen when I speak! You are thicker than a tall obelisk 100 cubits high and 10 cubits wide.

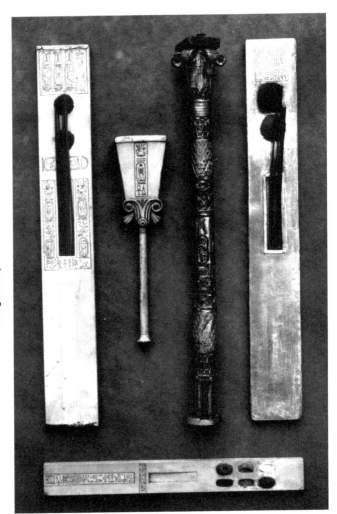

34. Tutankhamun's writing implements, found in his tomb, show the high status of the scribe in ancient Egypt – higher than in Mesopotamia

Another work portrays a father taking his son to school and advising him to be diligent if he is to avoid a life of backbreaking manual labour. 'I have seen the smith at his work beside his furnace,' the father declares. 'His fingers are like crocodile skin, and he stinks worse than fish roe.' Then the father disparages each manual trade in turn. Yet another papyrus concludes: 'The profession of scribe is a princely profession. His writing materials and his rolls of books bring pleasantness and riches.'

Clay, papyrus, and paper

By far the majority of cuneiform inscriptions are written on clay. To produce a good clay tablet must have been one of the first tasks of an apprentice scribe. The largest tablets had eleven columns and could be 30 centimetres square. One side was generally flat, the obverse side remained convex. The scribe wrote first on the flat side, and when this was full, he turned the tablet over and wrote on the curved side; the first set of signs, being flat, was therefore undamaged by pressure.

When finished, a tablet was usually left to dry out; such tablets could be altered by moistening the clay. Instead, a tablet might be baked, to create a permanent record. If this happened inadvertently in a fire, during the destruction of a library, it might preserve the tablet in perpetuity. Tablets baked in fires are mostly dark grey or black, while those baked today for their better preservation, are dark orange-brown. So-called 'firing holes' were sometimes made in the tablet by pressing a stylus (or similar object) right through (or almost through) the clay. Scholars formerly supposed that these holes were to help the tablet dry out or to stop it from fracturing when baked, but some large tablets were successfully baked without the use of holes. It seems that firing holes, whatever their original purpose was, soon became a matter of tradition: there are copies of literary texts in which the firing holes in the original text have been meticulously preserved in the copy.

When inscribing a tablet, a scribe would start at the top left-hand edge, work downwards to the bottom edge, return to the top of the next column and repeat the process, thus steadily moving to the right of the tablet in columns. On reaching the bottom right-hand corner, he would turn the tablet over on its bottom edge, begin writing in the top right-hand corner and work leftwards in columns. So clay tablets were written and read as we read a modern newspaper, except that the ancient scribes turned over the 'page' along the bottom edge, rather than the side edge.

The stylus was usually made of reed, though occasionally it was of metal or bone. Reed was common in the marshlands of the Near East, and had strength. A scribe could easily trim a reed to give a circular end, a pointed end, a flat end, or a diagonally cut end. Each shape had its uses, such as impressing the numerals with the circular end (see photograph 1 below), and some reed shapes generated recognizable styles of scribal hand.

The stylus could obviously be oriented in any direction the scribe wanted, in relation to the tablet; and if the tablet was small enough, it too could be turned back and forth in the hand. In practice, only a limited range of sign angles was used. A study of any cuneiform inscription reveals that individual wedges seldom point upwards, to the left, or slant up the right. (Forgers tend to miss this fact.) We can see why, if we consider how the tablet was held. Assuming that most scribes were right-handed, the tablet was held between

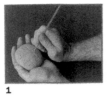 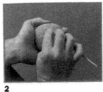 

1   **2**   **3**

35. Cuneiform was written on a clay tablet with a reed stylus shaped to make various kinds of sign. See the text for a fuller explanation

thumb and fingers. In this position a variety of wedges could be made, but many possible wedges are awkward. We find that the first angle of wedge (photograph 2) is commonly found in later cuneiform, while the second angle (photograph 3) is rare and disappeared from standard usage in about 2300 BC.

The word 'paper', which is attested in English since the 14th century, is derived from the Latin word for papyrus, which itself seems to derive from the Egyptian 'pa-en-per-aa', meaning 'that which belonged to the king'. (Most likely, papyrus was manufactured and issued under royal monopoly.) But although papyrus has an arguable claim to be the world's first paper, a distinction is normally drawn between papyrus and paper in modern usage.

Sheets of papyrus were made by stripping and slicing up sections of the stems of the papyrus plant found in the Nile Delta. Many thin, soaked strips of the pith were then overlapped in layers at right angles to each other; the layers were pressed together so that the gluey sap ensured adhesion; and the strips were left to dry into strong and flexible sheets. Sheets could then be stuck together to make long rolls; the side with horizontally laid fibres had to be on top to ensure that the sheet, when rolled, did not crack on the written side. The oldest known of these rolls, which is uninscribed, was found in the 1st dynasty tomb of Hemaka at Saqqara, dating to 3035 BC.

Sheets of paper, by contrast, were derived from cotton, flax, wood, and other plant materials, which had been treated with water and sometimes heat, and then beaten into a pulp to release the cellulose fibres. These were collected as a mat on a woven screen, compressed, and dried into sheets. (Various chemicals are now added during this process, for whitening and coating to reduce absorbency.)

Credit for discovering how to make paper is traditionally given to Cai Lun, a eunuch at the imperial court in China. In AD 105, he is said to have made 'zhi', defined by a contemporary dictionary as 'a mat of refuse fibres', from tree bark, the remnants of hemp, rags of cloth, and old fishing nets. But archaeological evidence, in the form of very early specimens of paper found at several arid sites in western China, suggests that paper-making probably started earlier than this, during the 2nd century BC, in the tropical regions of south and southeast China. It is even possible it began in the 6th or 5th century BC, when the washing of hemp and linen rags is attested; someone might have stumbled on the possibilities while drying some wet refuse fibres on a mat.

From China, the idea of paper reached Korea, Vietnam, and Japan, which were producing their own paper within a few centuries. Its diffusion to far-off Europe was much slower; paper was not made there for nearly a millennium. The idea followed the Silk Route – there are merchants' letters written on paper found near Dunhuang in the far west of China, dating to the 4th to 6th centuries AD – and was transmitted to Europe via the Arab rulers and Islamic civilization. In the 11th century, the Moorish rulers of Spain established paper mills and introduced Christian Europe to the ancient Chinese invention.

Calligraphy

'Calligraphy' means originally 'beautiful writing' (from the ancient Greek). It has been practised in all literate cultures and periods, from the Egyptian hieroglyphs and the Book of the Dead, through illuminated medieval Western manuscripts like the Lindisfarne Gospels, to today's elaborate wedding invitations. But it has been particularly important in modern times in the Arab world and in China.

With the coming of Islam and the rise of the Arabic script in the 7th century AD, the artistic spirit of the Arabs went into calligraphy and abstract decoration, because of the general Muslim reluctance to paint pictures with religious imagery. The particular esteem accorded to the copying of the Koran gave calligraphy great prestige. It also gave rise to dominant styles of writing the Arabic script, notably Kufic and then Naskhi, and Maghribi, used in North Africa. Persia and Ottoman Turkey developed other significant styles for writing vernacular Arabic.

Certain features of the Arabic script dictate its calligraphic appearance. There are the diacritics – dots and short strokes – placed above and below consonants to indicate vowels; and the fact that certain letters may be joined to their neighbours, other letters only to the preceding one, and still other letters only to the succeeding one. Also important is that there are no capital forms of letters. In addition, the Arabic calligrapher writes with a reed pen with its point cut at an angle, which produces a thick downstroke, a thin upstroke, and an infinity of gradations between.

In China, calligraphy has always been more than simply refinement or elaboration of writing; it has been synonymous with writing. The Chinese do not speak of 'fine handwriting', but simply of 'the art of writing', 'shufa'. In classical China, writing ('shu') was an art on a par with painting, poetry, and music, sometimes even above them.

For this reason, the Chinese calligrapher works not with a pen, but with a brush, like a painter. The hairs of Chinese brushes, which are generally inserted into bamboo handles, are of goat, hare, or marten. The hairs of wild martens shot in autumn are especially prized for their brisk reaction to changes of pressure, which imparts a spiritedness to the writing of Chinese characters.

There is, of course, a unique variety of forms in the Chinese script, as compared to alphabetic scripts. Chinese calligraphers are naturally challenged to use their brushes to express this variety aesthetically, while remaining legible – a crucial requirement. They aim to endow the Chinese characters with life, to animate them without distorting their fundamental shapes. In doing so, the calligrapher's artistic personality enters into the forms in a way that is not true of Western calligraphy, which is on the whole impersonal. The names of the greatest Chinese calligraphers, such as Wang Hsi-chih (died AD 379), are well known in China, unlike those of calligraphers in the West. Many great pieces of calligraphy, particularly from earlier periods, have four or five or even more autographs appended to them by later calligraphers, who thereby express their joy at the original master's achievement.

Chapter 9
Writing goes electronic

As the 6th millennium of recorded civilization opened, Mesopotamia was again at the centre of historical events. Once, at the birth of writing, the statecraft of absolute rulers like Hammurabi and Darius was written in Akkadian, Babylonian, Assyrian, and Old Persian cuneiform on clay, stone, and metal with a stylus. Now, the Iraq wars against Saddam Hussein generated millions of mainly alphabetic words written in a babel of world languages on paper and on the World Wide Web with an electronic computer. Yet although today's technologies of writing are immeasurably different from the tablets of the 3rd millennium BC, its linguistic principles have not changed very much since the composition of the Sumerian epic of Gilgamesh, generally regarded as the world's first literature.

Even text messaging by mobile phone – whether in English or Chinese – uses the concepts of phoneticism, logography, rebus, and abbreviation that were already in use in ancient Mesopotamia (not to mention the Arabic numerals). In English, 'before' is texted as 'b4'. In German, 'gute Nacht' is sent as 'gn8', since the numeral 8 is pronounced *acht* in German. In Japanese, 'san-kyu' (meaning 'thank you') is texted as '39', since the numeral 3 is pronounced *san* and the numeral 9 as *kyu* in Japanese – one of the numerous disconcerting examples of 'English' loanwords used in non-English text messages. In Chinese, text messagers have to be fanatically dedicated, given the obstacles presented by the character script. Chinese mobile phone users have an ingenious multi-key-press system used for creating characters, based on the number of strokes used to build up a character, which belong to a small number of groups learned in school. 'These groups are linked to locations on the mobile phone, so, by pressing the keys in the order in which the strokes would be drawn on paper, it is possible to build up the required character', explains the linguist David Crystal in his book *Txting: The Gr8 Db8*. Alternatively, Chinese texters can use Pinyin, the romanized system for writing Chinese phonetically, to select the characters.

Computing and the internet have had a seismic impact on written information, without an iota of doubt. Writing (and images) can be electronically created, edited, published, accessed, stored, and researched with an ease, reach, and cheapness that is still almost miraculous to those of us, like myself, who began writing on typewriters in the 1980s.

Even the printed book may be under threat. Will it go the way of the clay tablet, the papyrus roll, and the codex, during the 21st century? The publishing industry is currently divided on this issue. A survey of publishers in 2008, conducted by the Frankfurt Book Fair, showed that almost half expected the sale of digital content to outstrip sales of printed books within ten years, while one third expected that print would always dominate. I myself am inclined to agree with the second group (while fearing for the future of the reading habit). Books of all kinds have been one of the items most successfully traded on the World Wide Web from its earliest days. Educational book publishing has boomed in step with the growth in online learning. As the book review editor of a higher-education newspaper during this period, I was surprised by the ever-increasing stream of ever-expanding textbooks sent by publishers for review, even as their authors and publishers poured resources

36. Electronic text messaging is as language-dependent as any other form of full writing. Ancient Mesopotamians used abbreviations too

into compact discs, DVDs, and websites as companions for those printed titles.

The technological revolution in information has polarized the old debate about the correct definition of 'writing', too. Must 'full' writing depend on a spoken language, as maintained in this book? Or can it float free of its phonetic anchor?

The flourishing of the internet appears to suggest that the dream of universal communication across the barriers of language, nation, and culture by means of writing is within reach. Three centuries ago, in 1698, the philosopher and mathematician Gottfried Wilhelm Leibniz (inventor of the calculus) wrote: 'As regards signs, I see ... clearly that it is to the interest of the Republic of Letters and especially of students, that learned men should reach agreement on signs.' But the nature of full writing means that Leibniz's vision remains an impossible illusion. There is no such thing as a universal writing system, and there never will be.

In the mid-1970s, with increasing international travel, the American Institute of Graphic Arts cooperated with the United States Department of Transportation to design a set of symbols for airports and other travel facilities that would be clear both to travellers in a hurry and those without a command of English. They came up with 34 iconic symbols. The design committee made a significant observation. They wrote:

> We are convinced that the effectiveness of symbols is strictly limited. They are most effective when they represent a service or concession that can be represented by an object, such a bus or bar glass. They are much less effective when used to represent a process or activity, such as Ticket Purchase, because the [latter] are complex interactions that vary considerably from mode to mode and even from carrier to carrier.

The designers concluded that symbols should not be used alone, they must be incorporated as part of 'an intelligent total sign system', involving both symbols and alphabetic messages. To do otherwise would be to sow 'confusion' among air travellers.

Pictographic and logographic signs at airports and beside highways are a limited language of universal communication, which belongs to proto-writing, not full writing. Mathematics, too, is a universal language, but it is no use for most purposes of written communication. Comics and cartoons can be enjoyed by people speaking different languages, who cannot follow the captions and speech bubbles, but only very partially. Painting and music communicate powerfully across cultures, but their meaning is diffuse and ambiguous. To communicate 'any and all thought' always requires phonetic symbols. The popular online encyclopedia Wikipedia may have started in English – the chief language of the internet – but it subsequently evolved versions written in over two dozen languages, including Esperanto, the artificial language hopefully devised in 1887 as a medium of communication for persons of all languages. Full writing and reading depend on knowing a spoken language. This fact has not been altered by the internet – however many computer icons (and emoticons) we may encounter online.

Shorthand

If a universal writing system were possible, we might expect that the designers of shorthand would have approximated it, so that one

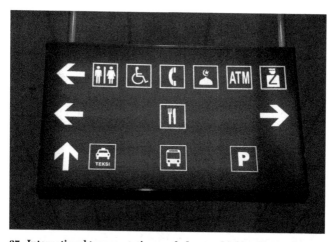

37. International transportation symbols are a highly effective form of proto-writing, which can never develop into full writing

set of shorthand symbols and rules could be used across the world. In fact, the history of shorthand is dominated by phonetic not logographic representation, based on individual languages.

Over 400 shorthand systems have been devised for writing the English language alone. The best known was invented by Isaac Pitman in the 19th century. Its basic principle is robustly phonetic, which makes it relatively easy to adapt for writing languages other than English. Some 65 letters are used, consisting of 25 single consonants, 24 double consonants, and 16 vowel sounds. However, most vowels are omitted, though they may be indicated by the positioning of a word above, on or below the line. The signs are a mixture of straight lines, curves, dots, and dashes – with not a hint of pictography as well as a contrast in positioning and shading. They relate to the sound system; for example, straight lines are used for all stop consonants (such as p), and signs for all labial consonants (such as f) slope backwards. The thickness of a line indicates whether a sound is voiceless or voiced.

The shorthand used by Samuel Pepys for writing his famous diary in the 17th century was much less phonetic than Pitman's. Invented by Thomas Shelton in the 1620s, in some ways it resembled an ancient writing system, such as Babylonian cuneiform, mixing phonetic signs with logograms and some redundant signs. Although many of the signs were simply reduced forms of English letters and abbreviations for English words, there were nearly 300 invented symbols, mainly arbitrary logograms, such as 2 for 'to', a large 2 for 'two', 5 for 'because', 6 for 'us'. (Several of these symbols were 'empty', presumably to foster the secrecy of the work.) Initial vowels were symbolized; medial vowels were indicated by placing the consonant following the vowel in five positions on, below or to the side of the preceding consonant; and final vowels were shown by dots, arranged similarly. Overall, the system was quasi-phonetic. Shelton's shorthand was popular in its day for reporting sermons and speeches, perhaps as fast as a hundred words per minute – but unlike Pitman's phonetic system, it did not endure.

The future of writing systems

Until the last few decades, it was generally agreed that over the centuries Western civilization had tried to make writing a closer and closer representation of speech. The alphabet was naturally regarded as the pinnacle of this conscious search; the Chinese script, conversely, was widely thought of as hopelessly defective. The corollary was the belief that as the alphabet spread through the world, so eventually would mass literacy and democracy. Surely, one might think, if a script is easy to learn, then more people will grasp it; and if they come to understand public affairs better, they will be more likely to take part in them and indeed demand a part in them. Scholars – at least Western scholars such as Ignace Gelb in *A Study of Writing* (1952) – thus had a clear conception of writing progressing from cumbersome ancient scripts with multiple signs to simple and superior modern alphabets.

Few are now quite as confident. The superiority of alphabets is no longer taken for granted. More fundamentally, the supposed pattern of a deepening perception of phonetic efficiency producing an increasing simplicity of orthography, is not borne out by the evidence. The ancient Egyptians, for example, had an 'alphabet' of 24 signs nearly 5,000 years ago, but apparently chose not to use it alone, and instead developed a logoconsonantal system with over 700 signs in regular use. The Japanese, rather than using their simple syllabic kana more and more frequently, chose to import more and more kanji from the Chinese script, creating a writing system of unrivalled complexity. Mayan glyphs show that the Maya could have used far more purely syllabic spellings, if they had wished, instead of their elaborate logographic and logosyllabic equivalents. The Aztecs appear to have deliberately refrained from developing the undoubted phonetic elements attached to their complex system of pictorial symbols and logograms into a fully fledged system of phonetic writing for their language Nahuatl.

Lastly, we might mention the notorious irregularity of modern English spelling, which is by no means a logical and straightforward representation of speech. The writer George Bernard Shaw, irritated by illogical English orthography, left money in his will to invent a rational alphabet for spelling English. A public competition drew 467 entries in 1958. Yet the winning entry, by Kingsley Read, with 48 letters, though ingenious and simple to write, has never been used. It is almost impossible to imagine public acceptance of a wholesale change in English orthography of the kind that was introduced in Turkey in 1928, when the country changed from writing in the Arabic script to writing in the Roman alphabet, or in Korea, with the less abrupt changeover from Chinese characters to Hangul.

The reason why scripts flourish or vanish has more to do with political and cultural considerations than purely linguistic ones. Literacy concerns far more than merely learning how to read and write. A Japanese physics student once outlined for me the genuine linguistic disadvantages of writing only in kana, without kanji, and then added: 'After all, a long tradition cannot change like that. It will NEVER happen!!' In other words, writing Japanese in kanji is a key part of Japanese identity. The Aztecs, by contrast, gradually abandoned their writing system in the century or two after the ruthless Spanish conquest of Mexico, and began writing in the Roman alphabet. Yet they changed their system not on linguistic grounds, because it was inferior or unable to compete with the alphabet, argues the leading Aztec writing expert Alfonso Lacadena, 'but as a consequence of the progressive disintegration of the cultural universe that sustained it'.

Many scholars of writing today have an increasing respect for the intelligence behind ancient scripts. Down with the monolithic 'triumph of the alphabet', they say, and up with Chinese characters,

Egyptian hieroglyphs, and Mayan glyphs, with their hybrid mixtures of pictographic, logographic, and phonetic signs. Their conviction has in turn nurtured a new awareness of writing systems as being enmeshed within societies, rather than viewing them somewhat aridly as different kinds of technical solution to the problem of efficient visual representation of a particular language. While I personally remain sceptical about the expressive virtues of pictograms and logograms, this growing holistic view of writing systems strikes me as a healthy development that reflects the real relationship between writing and society in all its subtlety and complexity. The transmission of my intimate thoughts to the minds of others in many cultures via intricate marks on a piece of paper or a computer screen, continues to amaze me as a kind of barely explicable magic.

Chronology

Ice Ages	Proto-writing, i.e. pictographic communication, in use
8000–1500 BC	Clay 'tokens' in use as counters, Middle East
from 3300 BC	Sumerian clay accounting tablets, Uruk, Iraq
from 3100 BC	Cuneiform script, Mesopotamia; hieroglyphic script, Egypt
from 2500 BC	Indus Valley seal inscriptions, Pakistan/northwest India
1900–1500 BC	Alphabet begins in Egypt, Palestine, and Sinai
from 1750 BC	Linear A script, Crete
1792–1750 BC	Hammurabi, king of Babylon, reigns
from 1450 BC	Hittite (Luvian) hieroglyphic script, Anatolia
1450–1200 BC	Linear B script, Crete/Greece
14th century BC	Alphabetic cuneiform script, Ugarit, Syria
1361–1352 BC	Tutankhamun reigns, Egypt
1200 BC	Oracle bone inscriptions in Chinese characters

from 1000 BC	Phoenician alphabet, Mediterranean
900 BC	Olmec inscriptions, Mexico
from 730 BC	Greek alphabet
from 8th century BC	Etruscan alphabet, northern Italy
from 650 BC	Demotic script, derived from hieroglyphic, Egypt
521–486 BC	Darius reigns; creates Behistun inscription, Iran
400 BC	Ionian alphabet becomes standard Greek alphabet
c. 270–c. 232 BC	Ashoka creates rock edicts in Brahmi and Kharosthi scripts, northern India
221 BC	Qin dynasty reforms Chinese character spelling
196 BC	Rosetta Stone inscription, Egypt
1st century AD	Dead Sea Scrolls in Hebrew/Aramaic script, Palestine
75	Latest cuneiform inscription
2nd century or before	Paper invented, China
from 2nd century	Maya glyphic script, Mexico; Runic alphabet, northern Europe
394	Latest Egyptian hieroglyphic inscription
615–683	Pacal, Classic Maya ruler, reigns, Mexico
712	*Kojiki*, earliest work of Japanese literature (in Chinese characters)
before 800	Printing invented, China
from 9th century	Glagolitic and Cyrillic alphabets (Slavonic scripts)
1440s	Sejong, king of Korea, creates Hangul script
15th century	Movable type invented, Europe
1560s	De Landa records Mayan 'alphabet'

1821	Sequoyah creates Cherokee 'alphabet', USA
1823	Egyptian hieroglyphic deciphered by Champollion
from 1840s	Mesopotamian cuneiform deciphered by Rawlinson and others
1867	Typewriter invented
1899	Oracle bone inscriptions discovered, China
1900	Cretan Linear A and B discovered
1905	Proto-Sinaitic inscriptions discovered, Sinai
1920s	Indus civilization discovered
1940s	Electronic computers invented
1948	Hebrew becomes a national language, Israel
1952	Linear B deciphered by Ventris
from 1950s	Mayan glyphs deciphered by Knorosov and others
1958	Pinyin alphabetic spelling, China
1980s	Electronic word-processor invented
1990s	World Wide Web (www) invented

Further reading

Chapter 1: Writing and its emergence

Daniels, Peter T. and William Bright (eds.), *The World's Writing Systems* (New York: Oxford University Press, 1996)

DeFrancis, John, *Visible Speech: The Diverse Oneness of Writing Systems* (Honolulu: University of Hawaii Press, 1989)

Nissen, Hans J., Peter Damerow, and Robert K. Englund, *Archaic Bookkeeping: Writing and Techniques of Economic Administration in the Ancient Near East* (Chicago: University of Chicago Press, 1993)

Postgate, Nicholas, Tao Wang, and Toby Wilkinson, 'The evidence for early writing: utilitarian or ceremonial?', *Antiquity*, 69 (1995): 459–80

Robinson, Andrew, *The Story of Writing: Alphabets, Hieroglyphs and Pictograms*, rev. edn. (London: Thames & Hudson, 2007)

Schmandt-Besserat, Denise, *Before Writing: From Counting to Cuneiform* (Austin: University of Texas Press, 1992)

Chapter 2: Development and diffusion of writing

Houston, Stephen D. (ed.), *The First Writing: Script Invention as History and Process* (Cambridge: Cambridge University Press, 2004); includes Jerrold S. Cooper, 'Babylonian beginnings: the origin of the cuneiform writing system in comparative perspective'

Martinez, Ma. del Carmen Rodriguez et al., 'Oldest writing in the New World', *Science*, 313 (15 September 2006): 1610–14 (and follow-up letter in *Science*, 315 (9 March 2007): 1365–6)

Powell, Marvin A., 'Three problems in the history of cuneiform writing: origins, direction of script, literacy', *Visible Language*, 15 (autumn 1981): 419–40

Trustees of the British Museum (no editor, six authors with an introduction by J. T. Hooker), *Reading the Past: Ancient Writing from Cuneiform to the Alphabet* (London: British Museum Press, 1990); contains 'Cuneiform' by C. B. F. Walker, 'Egyptian Hieroglyphs' by W. V. Davies, 'Linear B and Related Scripts' by John Chadwick, 'The Early Alphabet' by John F. Healey, 'Greek Inscriptions' by B. F. Cook, 'Etruscan' by Larissa Bonfante

Chapter 3: Disappearance of scripts

Baines, John, John Bennet, and Stephen Houston (eds.), *The Disappearance of Writing Systems: Perspectives on Literacy and Communication* (London: Equinox, 2008); includes David Brown, 'Increasingly redundant: the growing obsolescence of the cuneiform script in Babylonia from 539 BC'

Bonfante, Giuliano and Larissa Bonfante, *The Etruscans: An Introduction*, rev. edn. (Manchester: Manchester University Press, 2002)

Guy, Jacques B. M., 'General properties of the Rongorongo writing', *Rapa Nui Journal*, 20:1 (2006): 53–66

Chapter 4: Decipherment and undeciphered scripts

Coe, Michael D., *Breaking the Maya Code*, rev. edn. (New York: Thames & Hudson, 1999)

Parpola, Asko, *Deciphering the Indus Script* (Cambridge: Cambridge University Press, 1994)

Pope, Maurice, *The Story of Decipherment: From Egyptian Hieroglyphs to Maya Script*, rev. edn. (London: Thames & Hudson, 1999)

Robinson, Andrew, *The Last Man Who Knew Everything: Thomas Young* (New York: Pi Press, 2006)

Robinson, Andrew, *Lost Languages: The Enigma of the World's Undeciphered Scripts*, rev. edn. (London: Thames & Hudson, 2009)

Robinson, Andrew, *The Man Who Deciphered Linear B: The Story of Michael Ventris* (London: Thames & Hudson, 2002)

Chapter 5: How writing systems work

Coulmas, Florian, *The Blackwell Encyclopedia of Writing Systems* (Oxford: Blackwell, 1996)

Gaur, Albertine, *A History of Writing*, 3rd edn. (London: British Library, 1992)

Gelb, I. J., *A Study of Writing*, rev. edn. (Chicago: University of Chicago Press, 1963)

Unger, J. Marshall, *Ideogram: Chinese Characters and the Myth of Disembodied Meaning* (Honolulu: University of Hawaii Press, 2004)

Chapter 6: Alphabets

Diringer, David, *The Alphabet: A Key to the History of Mankind*, vols. 1 and 2, 3rd edn. (London: Hutchinson, 1968)

Mafundikwa, Saki, *Afrikan Alphabets: The Story of Writing in Afrika* (New York: Mark Batty, 2007)

Page, R. I., *Runes* (London: British Museum Press, 1987)

Powell, Barry B., *Homer and the Origin of the Greek Alphabet* (Cambridge: Cambridge University Press, 1991)

Chapter 7: Chinese and Japanese writing

DeFrancis, John, *The Chinese Language: Fact and Fantasy* (Honolulu: University of Hawaii Press, 1984)

Hessler, Peter, 'Oracle bones', *New Yorker* (16 and 23 February 2004): 118–31

Moore, Oliver, *Chinese* (London: British Museum Press, 2000)

Seeley, Christopher, *A History of Writing in Japan* (Leiden: E. J. Brill, 1991)

Chapter 8: Scribes and materials

Coe, Michael D. and Justin Kerr, *The Art of the Maya Scribe* (London: Thames & Hudson, 1997)

Safadi, Y. H., *Islamic Calligraphy* (London: Thames & Hudson, 1978)

Tsien, Tsuen-Hsuin, *Written on Bamboo and Silk*, 2nd edn. (Chicago: University of Chicago Press, 2004)

Wilkinson, Richard H., *Reading Egyptian Art: A Hieroglyphic Guide to Ancient Egyptian Painting and Sculpture* (London: Thames & Hudson, 1992)

Chapter 9: Writing goes electronic

Crystal, David, *Txtng: The Gr8 Db8* (Oxford: Oxford University Press, 2008)

Harris, Roy, *The Origin of Writing* (London: Duckworth, 1986)

Lacadena, Alfonso, 'Regional scribal traditions: methodological implications for the decipherment of Nahuatl writing', *PARI Journal*, 8 (spring 2008): 1–22

Taylor, Insup and David R. Olson (eds.), *Scripts and Literacy: Reading and Learning to Read Alphabets, Syllabaries and Characters* (Dordrecht: Kluwer, 1995)

Index

Expand your collection of
VERY SHORT INTRODUCTIONS

ARCHAEOLOGY
A Very Short Introduction
Paul Bahn

This entertaining Very Short Introduction reflects the
enduring popularity of archaeology – a subject which
appeals as a pastime, career, and academic discipline,
encompasses the whole globe, and surveys 2.5 million
years. From deserts to jungles, from deep caves to
mountain tops, from pebble tools to satellite photo-
graphs, from excavation to abstract theory, archaeology
interacts with nearly every other discipline in its attempts
to reconstruct the past.

'very lively indeed and remarkably perceptive ... a quite
brilliant and level-headed look at the curious world of
archaeology'
Barry Cunliffe, University of Oxford

'It is often said that well-written books are rare in archaeology, but this is a model of good writing for a general
audience. The book is full of jokes, but its serious
message – that archaeology can be a rich and fascinating subject – it gets across with more panache than any
other book I know.'
Simon Denison, editor of *British Archaeology*

www.oup.co.uk/vsi/archaeology